More Praise for *Leadership the Hard Way*

"Dov Frohman is a giant of Israeli high tech. His book isn't only about leadership, it is about the human spirit and how high it can soar. Frohman and Howard capture the expansive vision and non-stop creativity that have made Israel one of the most advanced centers of high-tech innovation in the world."

—Yossi Vardi, chairman, International Technologies; founding investor, Mirabillis Ltd., creator of ICQ

"From an early age, Frohman learned to transform fear of survival into courageous action. Some lessons for leaders: stick to your principles, welcome intelligent dissent, take time to daydream but then make your dreams real. This book will stimulate you to reflect on your practice of leading people."

—Michael Maccoby, author of *The Gamesman* and *The Leaders We Need, And What Makes Us Follow*

"Dov Frohman distills thirty years of experience on the front lines of the global economy—from Silicon Valley to Israel—in this beautifully written and compelling narrative. His wisdom is not just for business leaders, it's for anyone seeking to lead in today's tumultuous environment."

—AnnaLee Saxenian, dean of the School of Information, UC Berkeley; author of *The New Argonauts: Regional Advantage in a Global Economy*

Leadership the Hard Way

A WARREN BENNIS BOOK
This collection of books is devoted exclusively to new
and exemplary contributions to management thought
and practice. The books in this series are addressed to
thoughtful leaders, executives, and managers of all
organizations who are struggling with and committed
to responsible change. My hope and goal is to spark
new intellectual capital by sharing ideas positioned at
an angle to conventional thought—in short, to publish
books that disturb the present in the service of a
better future.

Books in the Warren Bennis Signature Series

Leadership the Hard Way

Why Leadership Can't Be Taught and How You Can Learn It Anyway

by Dov Frohman
with Robert Howard

JOSSEY-BASS
A Wiley Imprint
www.josseybass.com

Published by Jossey-Bass
A Wiley Imprint
989 Market Street, San Francisco, CA 94103-1741—www.josseybass.com

Jossey-Bass books and products are available through most bookstores. To contact Jossey-Bass directly call our Customer Care Department within the U.S. at 800-956-7739, outside the U.S. at 317-572-3986, or fax 317-572-4002.

Jossey-Bass also publishes its books in a variety of electronic formats. Some content that appears in print may not be available in electronic books.

Library of Congress Cataloging-in-Publication Data

Frohman, Dov, 1939-
 Leadership the hard way : why leadership can't be taught and how you can learn it anyway / Dov Frohman, Robert Howard. — 1st ed.
   p.   cm. — (The Warren Bennis series)
 Includes bibliographical references and index.
 ISBN 978-0-7879-9437-2 (cloth : alk. paper)
   1. Leadership. I. Howard, Robert, 1954- II. Title.
HD57.7.F757   2008
658.4'092—dc22

                                                             2008000874

Printed in the United States of America
FIRST EDITION
HB Printing   10 9 8 7 6 5 4 3 2 1

Contents

To the memory of my three sets of parents:

Abraham and Feijga Frohman, Amsterdam
Antonie and Jenneke Van Tilborgh, Sprang Capelle
Lea and Moshe Bentchkowsky, Tel Aviv

Foreword

Every now and then, a person of great wisdom and integrity comes along with a story that everyone needs to hear. Dov Frohman is such a person. As a maverick in the field of technology from the earliest days, Dov has been an innovator, a questioner, a radical, a champion, a sage, a survivor, and above all, a leader. He's never backed down from responsibility, and he's faced some hair-raising crises with unconventional methods and achieved undeniable results. Under his guidance, Intel Israel became a key part of the global company's success and helped make Israel a real player in the world's high-tech market.

Even if this were solely a book of his personal stories, it would be a very worthwhile read. These stories are highly engaging and provide an insider's view into one of the most competitive industries in the world, not to mention harrowing tales like his childhood spent in hiding in Nazi-occupied Holland or his decision to keep Intel Israel open during the first Gulf War, as Scuds were raining down around the country. It was a highly risky and controversial move, yet one characteristic of Dov's commitment to his company and his country.

Fortunately for us, however, this book is much more than a memoir. Dov's unique experiences have given him a perspective on leadership you won't find anywhere else, and he's spent many years reflecting on the most critical issues any leader or leader-to-be might encounter. This book is like having a personal mentor—someone who tells the truth about leadership, the good and the bad, the easy calls, and the thorny dilemmas. Dov has stood in the trenches, weathered the loneliness along with the accolades, and really dug deep into the role, and now we the readers get the benefit of his insights, which are by no means rote and always authentic. We rarely see this kind of transparency from our leaders, so take advantage of it while you can.

WARREN BENNIS
Santa Monica
January 2008

Introduction:
Flying Through a Thunderstorm

Few subjects have so preoccupied the business world in recent years as that of leadership. Witness the explosion of articles, books, training courses, and programs purporting to teach managers how to lead. Since the early 1990s, for example, the *Harvard Business Review* has published some 350 articles on the subject of leadership—135 of them since 2000 alone. Recently, one of the world's leading financial-services companies, Merrill-Lynch, began publishing an entire magazine devoted to the topic.[1] Initially targeted at the company's senior-management ranks, the magazine aims eventually to attract a broad senior-executive audience. And where business is going, the academy is never far behind. Leadership has blossomed into a whole new field of study. At some universities, you can even get a Ph.D. in it![2]

I'm sure there is at least some value in all these efforts. But I'm skeptical that they will produce more or better leaders. Indeed, at the very moment that we are seeing so many efforts to teach leadership, we are also experiencing widespread and continuous *failures* of leadership—and not just in business but in politics, education, and other institutions of modern society. Corporate fraud brings down high-flying companies such as Enron. CEOs are driven from office due to unethical, and probably illegal, practices involving the backdating of stock options. In the United States, at a time of new and unprecedented global crises, a so-called "MBA president" oversees what many see as one of the most incompetent and corrupt administrations in modern history. And in my native Israel, polls suggest that leading politicians and military leaders have lost the confidence of the nation over the way they sleep-walked into the 2006 summer war with Hezbollah. In short, there is a growing disconnect between our celebration of leadership and what appears to be our systematic inability to practice it.

In my opinion, a major reason for this disconnect is that most of the conventional wisdom about leadership today is, not *wrong* exactly, but surprisingly irrelevant to the true challenges and dilemmas of leading in today's economy and society. The claim of so many of the articles, books, and programs on the subject seems to be that leadership is largely a matter of technique, a set of skills that can be taught. If you read the right books or take the right training courses, it should be relatively easy—indeed, straightforward—to become a leader.

My thirty years on the front lines of the global economy have taught me that precisely the opposite is the case. I believe that learning how to lead is more in the nature of cultivating personal wisdom than it is of acquiring technical skills. No matter how much training you have or how many books you have read, nothing can fully prepare you for the challenge. In this respect, leadership isn't easy; it's difficult, necessarily difficult. And the most essential things about it cannot really be taught—although, in the end, they can be learned.

Thunderstorm Over Greece

I'm an active pilot, so allow me to draw an analogy with learning how to fly. When I decided in my fifties to become a pilot, I took lessons from the retired former head of Israel's Air Force Academy. He was in his late sixties at the time; he is still flying today in his eighties! A daredevil fighter pilot but a strictly by-the-book instructor, he taught me the basics, what I like to think of as "Flying 101": how to take off, navigate, read the instruments, make a landing, and so on. He gave me the confidence that I could actually do it. But he would never let me make my own mistakes.

Whenever I did something wrong, he would immediately take over and tell me what I needed to do to take corrective action. As a result, I may have learned the basics of flying, but my knowledge was abstract, and I was far from being an experienced pilot.

Later, when I bought a more advanced and technologically complex airplane, I had a second teacher who trained me on the avionic systems of my new plane. In contrast to my first teacher, he took a far more intuitive approach. When we went flying together, he seldom intervened in the process. Rather, he stressed a set of simple decision rules—and then let me go ahead, make my own mistakes, and figure out how to recover from them. This taught me how to start integrating the theory of flying with the practice of actually piloting a plane.

Yet neither of these teachers really prepared me for the moment I experienced a few years later when I was caught unexpectedly in a sudden thunderstorm over the southern coast of Greece. I was traveling with my family from our home in Jerusalem to our vacation home in the Dolomite Mountains of Italy. I had had my pilot's license for about four years and at the time was flying frequently, at least once or twice a week. So I felt confident about making the long trip. In addition, my son, who was twenty-five at the time, also had his pilot's license (although he was not qualified to fly the particular model of plane that I owned, a single-propeller Beechcraft Bonanza).

The first leg of the trip from Israel to the Greek island of Rhodes was uneventful. And when we took off from Rhodes en route to Corfu, where we were planning to spend the night, the weather was fine. But as we headed toward Athens, we encountered an unanticipated obstacle. The air traffic controller at the Athens airport informed us that there were flight restrictions for small planes over the Athens metropolitan area. So we had to change our flight plan and take a more southwesterly route skirting the southern coast of Greece's Peloponnesian peninsula.

My plane is equipped with a device known as a *stormscope*—an avionics instrument that looks like a radar screen and uses data from electrical discharge signals generated by lightning in the atmosphere to create a 360-degree map of areas of severe weather in the plane's vicinity. We began to notice indications on the stormscope of a major storm almost directly in our path, about fifty miles to the southwest and approaching quickly.

In a matter of minutes, the sky started clouding up. Soon heavy rain, and then hail, began hitting the windshield. Thunder pealed and long streaks of lightning shot across the sky. Before we knew it, we were in the middle of the storm. Enormous updrafts and downdrafts grabbed the plane, pulling it up and down two thousand to three thousand feet at a time. The turbulence was gut-wrenching. Helpless, I watched the altimeter circle furiously, first in one direction, then the next.

In his classic 1944 book about flying, *Stick and Rudder*, test pilot Wolfgang Langewiesche makes the observation that "what makes flying so difficult is that the flier's instincts—that is, his most deeply established habits of mind and body—will tempt him to do exactly the wrong thing."[3] The first impulse of an inexperienced pilot facing a sudden thunderstorm is to turn around and go back. Sometimes that can actually be the right thing to do—if you have sufficient advance warning. But if a storm comes up quickly, turning back can be dangerous. Turning requires banking, and banking accelerates the plane with the nose down. If the storm winds are strong enough, they can force you into a dive, causing the plane to stall and go into a spin. Without really thinking about it, I realized immediately that it was far too late for us to turn back. There was really no choice but to plow ahead.

Another common impulse when flying through a thunderstorm is to fight the turbulence, to try to correct the violent updrafts and downdrafts by pushing down (or pulling up) on the controls. But that is a critical mistake, because it can lead to such stress on the wings as to cause the breakup of the plane. Rather, surviving extreme turbulence requires another counterintuitive trick: instead of fighting the turbulence, a pilot needs to let it happen. Believe me, it is extremely difficult to consciously make this choice. We were flying over high mountains. I had no idea how low the downdrafts would take us. But there was nothing to do but just let it happen. I struggled simply to keep the wings level as the violent updrafts and downdrafts took their course.

After about fifteen minutes (which seemed like a lifetime) on this aerial roller-coaster ride, my son, who was monitoring the stormscope, saw a break in the storm to the northeast. We radioed Athens for a change in course, and within about five minutes things began to calm down. Then, with no warning, we shot out of the clouds, and almost as quickly as the storm had developed, it passed. We flew on, chastened but relieved, to Corfu. That night we learned from the news that a small Greek passenger jet, also caught in the storm, had experienced an especially violent drop of more than ten thousand feet. Five passengers who had neglected to fasten their seatbelts were killed.

In the years since, I have often wondered precisely how I got us through that storm. The answer is: I don't really know. To be sure, I had taken courses about flying in bad weather and had learned what to do and what not to do. But once I was in the middle of the storm, those lessons were far from my mind. There were too many contingencies to handle in too short a period of time to apply those lessons systematically. Instead, my reactions were immediate— rapid responses to the developments of the moment, driven by my realization that our very survival was at stake. We were skirting the brink of disaster, and all my energy and efforts were focused simply on getting us through. And, to be honest, there was also an element of luck involved.

An Environment of Turbulence

My point: leadership in today's economy is a lot like flying a plane through a thunderstorm. More and more organizations find themselves in an economic environment of nonstop turbulence. The social, economic, and technological sources of that turbulence are broadly familiar, but let me review them briefly here. First and foremost is the unrelenting pace of rapid technological change. "We live in an age in which the pace of technological change is pulsating ever faster, causing waves that spread outward toward all industries," former Intel CEO Andy Grove wrote more than ten years ago. "This increased rate of change will have an impact on you, no matter what you do for a living. It will bring new competition from new ways of doing things, from corners that you don't expect."[4]

With the rapid expansion and evolution of the Internet in the years since Grove wrote those words, they are more true than ever before. It's not just that business value increasingly flows to *innovation*—the ability to take risks and create fundamentally new ways of doing things. Even the most innovative companies sooner or later face what Harvard Business School professor Clayton Christensen has termed the "innovator's dilemma"—the supreme difficulty for those organizations that have succeeded at one generation of technology to continue to surf the wave of change and remain successful over subsequent generations of technology.[5]

Technologically driven turbulence is exacerbated by the ongoing globalization of the world economy. In one respect, of course, globalization is nothing new. Until quite recently, the world economy was probably more global in the first decade of the twentieth century than it has been at any time since. But whereas traditional globalization was dominated by a few centers of economic development that ruled over a vast periphery, today's globalization is different. Increasingly, the periphery is becoming the center. New players have sprung up in places that used to be on the far edge of the global economy. As they do, established companies are suddenly encountering new competitors that seem to come out of nowhere and appear almost overnight. Ten years ago, who would have thought that the world's largest steel company, Arcelor Mittal, would be owned by an Indian conglomerate? That IBM's PC business would be bought by a Chinese firm, Lenovo? Or that a tiny country like Israel would have more than seventy companies listed on the U.S. NASDAQ stock exchange—and attract twice as much venture capital investment as the entire European Union?

Since September 11, 2001, business leaders have become familiar with a third source of turbulence: new levels of geopolitical instability associated with global conflict, environmental catastrophe, terrorism, and war. The challenges that this instability poses for political leadership are dramatic (and, in my opinion, our political leaders—whether in the United States or in Israel—have not been equal to them). But they pose challenges to business leadership as well. The distinctive features of today's turbulent economy include not just rapid change but also growing uncertainty. Companies across the economy face new kinds of risks and new kinds of threats—not only to their organizations, but sometimes to the very lives of their employees.

It is precisely these forces of increased turbulence that have fueled the growing preoccupation with leadership. In such an environment, leadership isn't a luxury. It's a matter of survival. Yet the very forces that make leadership more critical also make teaching it extremely difficult (and, in its essentials, impossible). What it takes to successfully lead an organization through that turbulence is neither simple nor straightforward. There are too many contingencies to take into account, too much uncertainty. By definition, it can't be done "by the book." This is due in part to the inevitable gap between theory and practice. I believe there is always something of a disconnect between how we actually *do* leadership and how most so-called experts in the field talk about it. This gap is made even greater by the reality of turbulence. When circumstances are changing rapidly and outcomes are uncertain, planning, analysis, and theory can only take you so far.

In his book, Langewiesche describes a similar gap in most attempts to understand flying. He puts it this way: the problem with the so-called "Theory of Flight" is that "it usually becomes a theory of building the airplane rather than of flying it. It goes deeply—much too deeply for a pilot's needs—into problems of aerodynamics; it even gives the pilot a formula by which to calculate his lift! But it neglects those phases of flight that interest the pilot the most."[6] One of the purposes of Langewiesche's book is to bring the theory of flying closer to the actual practice. In these pages, I want to do something similar for leadership.

Another reason leadership can't be taught is that it is highly personal. At the moment of truth, when survival is at stake (literally, in that thunderstorm over the Peloponnese; figuratively, in the struggles of global business competition), leadership is a matter of courage: a willingness to take risks and do the unexpected; to make judgments with no data or, at best, inadequate data; to face one's fear of failure. Summoning up such courage is a highly personal act. Each leader does it differently—and you never know if you will be able to do it until the moment of truth arrives. For all the talk about "managing risk" (if I had known in advance that we wouldn't be able to fly over Athens, maybe I would have checked the weather on the southwesterly route more carefully, been forewarned about the storm, and taken steps to avoid it), every leader knows in his gut that you can't anticipate everything. Sometimes risks can't be managed; they simply must be lived.

Put simply, I believe that any genuine leader today has to learn leadership the hard way—through doing it. That means flying through the thunderstorm; embracing turbulence, not avoiding it; taking risks; trusting (but also testing) your intuitions; doing the unexpected. This is not to say that there are no basic principles to orient you to the challenge (indeed, I will describe some in this book). But there are no simple recipes. Until you have lived it, you don't really know how to do it. I call this perspective "leadership the hard way." It is the subject of this book.

A Self-Taught Leader

Despite the fact that leadership cannot be taught, some individuals do find a way to learn how to become leaders. In effect, they are self-taught. And one of the most useful resources for that self-teaching is the life stories of those who have already made the journey.

I never planned to become a leader. I never went to business school, and I never expected to run a business organization. And yet, perhaps precisely for that reason, I believe that my experience makes me especially well suited to describe what it takes to lead in a turbulent economy. For more than thirty years, I worked as an inventor, entrepreneur, manager, and global pioneer in one of the most volatile of global businesses, the semiconductor industry, and in one of the most dangerous regions of the world, the Middle East.

University of California researcher AnnaLee Saxenian has recently identified a new category of global business leaders. She calls them the "new Argonauts": individuals from the traditional periphery of the global economy who have migrated to developed economies, learned the disciplines of global business, and then returned to their home countries to build dynamic, state-of-the-art, globally competitive businesses.[7]

Without knowing it at the time, I was one of the first new Argonauts. I left Israel in the early 1960s to get a Ph.D. in electrical engineering at the University of California at Berkeley. I got in on the ground floor of what would come to be known as Silicon Valley, working first at Fairchild Semiconductor's R&D lab (a famous breeding ground for high-technology startups), then as one of the early employees at Intel Corporation after Robert Noyce and Gordon Moore left Fairchild to found the company in 1968. I even made my own contribution to the computer industry with my invention in 1971 of the EPROM (erasable programmable read-only memory). The EPROM was the first nonvolatile but reprogrammable semiconductor memory—an innovation that Moore termed "as important in the development of the microcomputer industry as the microprocessor itself."[8]

But my dream had always been to bring back a new body of knowledge to Israel and help found a new field of innovation and industry there. So in 1974 (after a detour teaching electrical engineering in Ghana), I returned to Israel to set up Intel's first overseas design and development center in Haifa. Few people know it, but we designed the microprocessor for the original IBM personal computer. And in 1985 we opened the company's first chip fabrication plant (or fab) outside the United States, in Jerusalem. Through the cyclical ups and downs of the semiconductor business and through at least two wars, I helped grow Intel Israel into a key global outpost of the Intel Corporation and an important player in Israel's high-tech economy. In the process, I helped spark the development of Israel's high-tech economy, which is currently the home of some 4,500 technology companies, more than 300 venture capital funds and investment firms, and a collection of startups that is second in size only to Silicon Valley itself.

I retired from Intel in 2001. Today, Intel Israel is the headquarters for the company's global R&D for wireless technology (it developed the company's Centrino mobile computing technology, which powers millions of laptops worldwide) and is responsible for designing the company's most advanced microprocessor products. It's also a major center for chip fabrication: although Intel Israel's original fab in Jerusalem finally closed its doors in March 2008, Intel has two major semiconductor fabs in the city of Qiryat Gat in the south of Israel on the edge of the Negev desert. With some seven thousand employees (projected to reach nearly ten thousand by 2008), Intel Israel is the country's largest private employer. In 2007, Intel Israel's exports totaled $1.4 billion and represented roughly 8.5 percent of the total exports of Israel's electronics and information industry (which themselves equaled about a quarter of Israel's total industrial exports—the highest percentage for high tech anywhere in the world).

But my story is not really about technology. As the international economy becomes more volatile and uncertain, I believe that my experience in the semiconductor business and in running a global business from Israel is relevant to managers across the economy. True, I can't teach you to be a leader. But I believe I can show you how to learn to become one: by describing my personal, hands-on encounter with the turbulence of the global economy.

A Different Kind of Leadership Book

Leadership the Hard Way is a different kind of book about leadership. First, it offers a perspective not from the center but from the dynamic edge of the new global economy. Second, it is a view of leadership from within, not from the top, of the global corporation (I don't believe you necessarily have to be a CEO to be a leader). Finally, and most important, it avoids simple recipes in favor of what the anthropologists call *thick description*: life stories that crystallize the lessons of one leader's lifetime learning how to lead.

For example, I will tell you how my childhood as a Jewish boy in hiding in Nazi-occupied Holland during World War II, my experience of the Berkeley counterculture in the 1960s, and the serendipitous process I went through to invent the EPROM all helped shape my approach to leadership. And I will use the story of the creation and development of Intel Israel to describe how I refined my approach and put it into practice. I tell these stories not to blow my own horn, but rather because no discussion of the challenges of leadership is complete without somehow communicating the daunting complexity of situations and the bewildering variety of contexts that real-life leaders face. It is only through such stories that one can begin to approach the fundamental paradox of leadership: the fact that, while it cannot be taught, it can nevertheless be learned.

The first part of the book explores three general principles of "leadership the hard way." In an environment of constant turbulence, where survival can no longer be taken for granted, the fundamental responsibility of the leader is to ensure the long-term survival of the organization. Chapter One explains why insisting on survival has become so central to the role of the leader—and how I tried to create a culture at Intel Israel in which the imperative of survival became a powerful catalyst for improvisation and innovation.

Survival in a fast-changing environment requires what I call "leading against the current," or constantly challenging an organization's conventional wisdom and preconceptions. In Chapter Two, I describe how I acted against the current to make Intel Israel into a distinctive counterculture within Intel Corporation and how, paradoxically, our counterintuitive perspective on the edge of the corporation allowed us to move to the very center of Intel's global strategy and operations.

Turbulence is also changing the very nature of opportunity—making it increasingly less predictable. Leadership the hard way therefore also requires the leader to be alert to the often random opportunities that exist in the midst of crisis and to move fast to exploit them. Chapter Three uses the story of how I created Intel Israel in the first place to describe the special qualities that leaders must cultivate in order to leverage random opportunities systematically.

Sooner or later, every leader faces a moment of truth, what Warren Bennis and Robert Thomas call a "crucible" experience that shapes you definitively as a leader.[9] Chapter Four tells the story of what was, without question, the biggest leadership test of my thirty-year career: my decision to keep Intel Israel open during the early days of the First Gulf War in 1991, when Saddam Hussein's Iraq was raining Scud missiles down on Israel and businesses across the country were closing at the recommendation of Israel's civil defense authority. The story may be an excellent case study of leadership under conditions of extreme turbulence. In the way that it illustrates the three principles described in the preceding chapters, it is also a compelling conclusion to the first half of the book.

Leadership the hard way is a demanding way of life. It demands a lot from the leader as an individual. It also demands a great deal from people in the organization. The second half of the book describes the support infrastructure that the leader and the organization need to put in place to meet these demands. For example, Chapter Five addresses some rarely discussed "soft skills of hard leadership"—distinctive habits of mind and modes of interaction with people that need to be in place for leadership the hard way to work. Chapter Six takes a fresh look at the much-discussed subject of values, arguing that perhaps the most important precondition for an organization to stay true to its values is the leader's openness and honesty when he himself falls short of them. Finally, the book concludes with some general reflections on the key resources for you, as an aspiring leader, to bootstrap your own leadership skills—despite the fact that no one (including me) can really teach you how to lead.

A beginning pilot at least has the advantage of using a flight simulator to approximate the turbulent conditions that occur during a thunderstorm. But it's impossible to create a simulator for leading a complex organization. No book can substitute for the live ammunition of actually leading through turbulence and crisis.

Yet my hope is that this book will get you thinking and give you some ideas for how to become a self-taught leader. Think of it as your own personal stormscope, alerting you to the challenges, dilemmas, and pitfalls—but also opportunities—ahead. Happy flying!

DOV FROHMAN
December 2007

Leadership the Hard Way

1

INSISTING ON SURVIVAL

In a turbulent economy, the first task of the leader is insisting on survival—that is, continuously identifying and addressing potential threats to the long-term survival of the organization. At first glance this statement may seem obvious, even trivial. Doesn't it go without saying that no organization can be successful if it doesn't first survive? Yet the rapid increase in the pace of change in business has made survival more problematic than ever before. The frequency with which organizations face major challenges to their survival is growing.

In the days when most established companies had relatively stable markets and competitors, survival was only rarely an issue. To be sure, every now and then a company might face a major crisis, but once that crisis was addressed, things went back to normal. Few companies today have that luxury. Threats to survival aren't occasional; they are nearly continuous. If an organization waits for a full-blown crisis to develop, it may find that it is already too late.

The growing frequency of threats to survival is especially evident in technology- or innovation-based businesses. In such businesses, success at any one generation of technology is really only buying an option on the future. It wins you the right to compete at the next level of technology, but offers no guarantees of continual success. Indeed, quite the opposite: often it is those companies that are most successful at one generation of technology that have the most difficulty in adapting to subsequent generations.

I believe it was the increasingly problematic nature of survival that Andy Grove had in mind when he claimed famously that "only the paranoid survive." As Grove describes in his book of that name, sooner or later, every business reaches what he calls a "strategic inflection point"—that "time in the life of a business when its fundamentals are about to change. That change can mean an opportunity to rise to new heights. But it may just as likely signal the beginning of the end."[1] Grove makes clear that such strategic inflection points can be caused by technological change but they are about more than just technology. They can be caused by new competitors, but they are about more than just the competition. "They are full-scale changes in the way business is conducted." As such they "can be deadly when unattended to."

Despite the proliferation of such threats to survival in business today, most people in most organizations avoid engaging squarely with the issue. This is partly a result of the complacency that comes with success. But even more, there is something in the very nature of an organization that leads its members to take its ongoing existence for granted. In this respect, an organization is a lot like an adolescent. It assumes it is going to live forever!

It's easy to understand why most people would prefer not to think about potential threats to their survival. It's scary, and fear can be paralyzing. Nobody wants to consider the possibility that "I might not survive!" What's more, threats to survival generate massive uncertainty. To survive such threats means to take risks. But risks are by definition uncertain. What if we try and fail? What if things don't work out? No wonder people avoid the issue of survival, if they can get away with it.

The job of the leader is to make sure they don't get away with it. A leader must represent to the organization the imperative of survival, the challenge of survival, and the reality of threats to survival. By constantly asking "What will it take to survive?" leaders in effect force people to anticipate *in advance* the potential threats facing the organization. In this way, they become the catalyst for continuous adaptation that allows the organization to avoid a genuine crisis of survival.

To do this effectively, you must take a position consciously "in opposition" to the organization and its identity and systematically resist the taken-for-grantedness that one finds in any organization.

The leader has to embody the possibility that the organization can fail and fail disastrously—precisely to make sure that it does not.

A Wartime Childhood

In retrospect, I realize that my preoccupation—some might say *obsession*—with survival is, at least in part, a by-product of my experience as a child during the Second World War. My parents, Abraham and Feijga Frohman, were Polish Jews who emigrated to Holland in the early 1930s to escape the rising anti-Semitism in Poland. I was born in Amsterdam on March 28, 1939, just months before the start of the war.

After the German invasion of the Low Countries in 1940, we continued to live in Amsterdam. But in 1942, as the Nazi grip on Holland's Jewish community steadily tightened, my parents made the difficult decision to give me up to people they knew in the Dutch underground, who hid me with a family in the Dutch countryside.

Antonie and Jenneke Van Tilborgh were devout Christians, members of the *Gereformeerde Kerk* or Calvinist Reformed Church, the most orthodox branch of Dutch Protestantism. They lived on a farm on the outskirts of Sprang Capelle, a small village in the region of Noord Braband, in southern Holland near the Belgian border. The Van Tilborghs had four children. Their oldest daughter, Rie, was twenty-one but still living at home. Another daughter, Jet, was fourteen. And the two boys, Coor and Toon, were ten and six. The Van Tilborgh family hid me from the Germans for the duration of the war. Only a few close neighbors knew that I was staying with them.

I was only three when I arrived at the Van Tilborgh household, so it is difficult to differentiate between what I actually remember and what I was told later. But one thing I do recall was feeling different. For example, I had dark hair, and the Van Tilborgh children were all blond. I had to wear a black hat to hide my black hair.

I also remember hiding when the Germans would search the village. Sometimes I would hide under the bed, sometimes in the root cellar (I have a warm memory of treating myself to the apples that were stored there), sometimes with my "brothers" and "sisters" out in the surrounding woods. To this day I have a scar on my wrist that, according to the Van Tilborghs, came from a time when we were running through the woods and I tried to jump over a creek and got caught by some barbed wire.

Other memories are more disturbing. One day, looking out the cellar window, I saw German soldiers execute a fellow soldier. I don't know why they were doing it; perhaps he was a deserter, perhaps he himself had helped some Jews who were in hiding. Whatever the cause, I have the image seared in my mind of seeing him hit by the bullets and falling to the ground in a heap.

My parents did not survive the war. They were taken in one of the many roundups of Jews by the Nazis. Much later, I learned that my father died in Auschwitz. I never learned for sure where my mother died, although it's likely she was taken to Auschwitz as well.

I see now that my experience during the war inculcated in me a stubborn conviction that nothing is truly secure, that survival must never be taken for granted—but also that the actions of determined individuals can "achieve the impossible" and have a literally heroic impact on events. If it weren't for my parents' ability to make the excruciatingly difficult choice to give me up to the underground and for the Van Tilborghs' willingness to take me in, I wouldn't be here today.

Who knows what motivates human beings to do something truly heroic? In the case of the Van Tilborghs, it is clear to me that a major source of their motivation was their deep religious faith. Without such bedrock convictions, they wouldn't have been able to do what they did. I also suspect that their own experience as members of a minority religious sect in Holland allowed them to empathize and identify with the plight of Holland's Jews and develop a compelling urgency to do something about it. Orthodox Calvinists made up only about 8 percent of the population of the Netherlands in the 1940s. Yet they were responsible for helping roughly a quarter of the approximately twenty-five thousand Jews who went into hiding. Thanks to the help of people like the Van Tilborghs, some sixteen thousand Jews who went into hiding survived the war, including some four thousand children like myself.[2]

In agreeing to hide me, the Van Tilborghs took unimaginable risks. They endangered not only themselves, but their own children as well—to a degree that, seen from the outside, may appear almost irresponsible. In contemplating their example over the years, I learned something essential about leadership: survival requires taking big risks, and sometimes the risks a leader takes, when viewed from a normal or conventional point of view, can appear crazy. But it really only looks that way. Often, genuine leadership is the result of the leader's commitment to a transforming vision and to a set of values that follow from that vision. A key challenge of leadership is to live with the tension between two incommensurate sets of values, perspectives, and commitments—in this particular case, the Van Tilborghs' responsibilities to their children and the responsibilities they took on in protecting me.

I also learned something else from the Van Tilborghs' behavior. If a leader is too focused on personal survival as head of the organization, he or she may end up, paradoxically, undermining the organization's long-term capacity to survive. A lot of ineffective leaders become so focused on their own survival in their leadership role that they avoid taking necessary risks and, in the long run, end up damaging the organization's survival capacity. Much like the Van Tilborghs who saved me during World War II, sometimes visionary leaders must risk themselves to do the right thing.

After the liberation of southern Holland in 1944, my father's sister, who had emigrated to Palestine in the 1930s, somehow was able to locate me. She had a friend who was serving in the Jewish Brigade—the volunteer fighting force of Palestinian Jews raised by the British that had fought in North Africa and Europe and that, at the time, was stationed in nearby Belgium. She sent the friend to meet with the Van Tilborghs and convince them to place me in a Jewish orphanage, with the intention of eventually emigrating to Palestine.

The Van Tilborghs were hesitant to let me go and, to be honest, I didn't want to leave. By that time I barely remembered my parents. For all intents and purposes, the Van Tilborghs had become my family. But after all that had happened to European Jewry during the war, the Jewish community was determined to recover those children who had survived. Eventually the Van Tilborghs were persuaded that it was the best thing for me and, reluctantly, they gave me up. I lived the next few years in orphanages for Jewish children whose parents had died during the war, first in Antwerp and then in Marseilles, before sailing to the newly created country of Israel on the *Theodore Herzl* in 1949.

Eventually I was adopted by relatives in Israel. But I never forgot the Van Tilborghs, and over the years I have kept in touch with my Dutch family. Antonie and Jenneke are dead now, as are two of their four children. But the families continue to keep in touch. The children of my Dutch brothers and sisters know my children. We have attended their weddings in Holland, and they have visited us in Israel, where Antonie and Jenneke's names are enrolled on the list of the Righteous Among the Nations in the records of Yad Vashem, Israel's official memorial to those who died in the Holocaust.

"The Last Operation to Close in a Crisis"

It may seem absurd, or perhaps even inappropriate, to compare the threats I faced as a young Jew in Nazi-occupied Europe to the competitive threats that most companies face today. Yet, in part because of my childhood experience, I've always believed that an organization's survival can never be taken for granted—in bad times certainly, but also even in good times. For this reason, it is essential for an organization to accept complete responsibility for its own survival.

When you're working in a startup, this responsibility is obvious. Every day you live with the possibility that you might not succeed. But when you are working in a large global corporation, it's easy to become passive, to assume that the company will be around forever, even to start thinking that your own fate relies on decisions made at corporate headquarters far away. When I founded Intel Israel, I was determined to fight this tendency, to cultivate the atmosphere of a precarious startup, even though we were part of a successful and fast-growing company. I wanted people not only to avoid complacency but also to feel that they—and they alone—were responsible for their own fate.

For that reason, my vision for Intel Israel always emphasized survival in a highly volatile industry and region. After all, semi-conductors is a highly cyclical business, with dizzying booms often followed by extremely painful busts. And in the 1970s and '80s, when we were building Intel Israel, Intel was passing through some of the most important and most dangerous strategic inflec-tion points of its history—in particular, the company's exit from the memory business in the mid-1980s. If that wasn't turbulence enough, we were also trying to build an outpost for Intel in the Middle East, a region wracked by political tension and war and that, despite moments of hope in the 1990s, still has not found its way to a definitive peace.

So I saw threats to survival everywhere and was determined to make sure we were tough enough to survive them. As I used to put it, I wanted Intel Israel to be "the last Intel operation to close in a crisis." To be honest, many employees, including some of my direct reports, didn't much like this vision. They thought it was too negative. "Is that the best we can do," they would ask, "just avoid being closed down?" Eventually we came up with a simple slogan: "Survival through success." And I used that slogan to drive our behavior in every area of the business.

Take the example of layoffs. Layoffs at Intel were relatively rare—but they did happen, especially in the company's early years. In 1970 the company had had to lay off 10 percent of its (then still quite small) workforce after the market failure of its very first product. In 1974 the first big downturn in the industry caused the company to lay off 30 percent of its workforce, about 350 people. And in 1986 there were plant closings and layoffs associated with exiting the memory business.

From the moment I helped establish Intel Israel, I simply refused to accept the idea that we would lay people off, and I went out of my way to make sure that whatever layoffs did occur at Intel as a whole happened to others, not to Intel Israel. Of course, the only sure way to avoid layoffs was to make sure that our operations were so competitive that they were "the last to close in a crisis." But sometimes more extraordinary measures were necessary.

In the 1990s, for example, we had a small software development group at the Haifa design center. But in 1994, in a move aimed to cut costs, the global head of Intel's systems software unit decided to close it down. To avoid losing what was a cadre of highly skilled software programmers, I immediately traveled to the States and met with Intel's then-CEO Andy Grove to see whether there was any way to fund their positions, at least temporarily, until other more long-term opportunities opened up.

I argued that these were highly skilled employees and to lay them off now, although it might be penny-wise, was certainly pound-foolish. Come the next upturn, we would need these people, so we should keep them with Intel. Grove agreed to commit some $700,000 to keep the people at Intel, and we distributed them among other engineering groups. The decision paid off three years later when, with the ramp-up to the Internet boom in the late 1990s, we found ourselves facing yet another shortage of software engineers. As a result of such efforts, there were fewer than ten employees who had to be laid off during my entire tenure at Intel Israel.

Containing Fear

Earlier I mentioned that people don't want to think about survival because it is scary. In fact, there is a complex relationship between survival and fear. To insist on survival, a leader must know how to navigate fear. The goal is neither to exaggerate fear nor to eliminate it, but rather to contain it.

It can be difficult for leaders to maintain this delicate balance. Take an example that is top of mind for so many people today—the fear of terrorism. In my opinion, many political leaders in both the United States and Israel aren't containing fear over terrorism so much as exacerbating it. Indeed, they exploit fear to further their political agenda. When you think about it, their message is completely contradictory: on the one hand, they exaggerate the "existential threat" of terrorism to keep people in a state of constant anxiety; on the other, they promise perfect security—on the condition, of course, that the public support their policies. Both are illusions. In a turbulent world, there is no such thing as perfect security. But at the same time, extreme fear leads only to passivity and paralysis, making it all the more difficult to address the genuine challenges that we face. Whether for terrorism or any of the other threats we face in today's world, it is more true than ever that "the only thing we have to fear is fear itself."

Yet it is impossible—and unwise—to eliminate fear completely. I disagree, for example, with the famous advice of quality guru Edward Deming that leaders must "banish fear" from the organization. This viewpoint strikes me as unrealistic. In situations in which survival is at stake, a certain degree of fear is inevitable. Indeed, a healthy fear of failure can be a good—indeed, even an essential—thing. It helps break through organizational complacency (it certainly kept me focused when confronting that thunderstorm over the coast of Greece). With the right amount of fear, people perform better because nobody wants to fail.

So leaders have to master a delicate balancing act. On the one hand, they must acknowledge the inevitable fear that survival situations engender; admit that, in a turbulent world, perfect security is not achievable; and, indeed, use that realistic fear to keep people on their toes. But at the same time, they also must contain the fear, keep it from paralyzing people, encourage risk taking, and mobilize the organization to rise to the occasion when its very survival is threatened. I call this "worst-case thinking"—always trying to anticipate what can go wrong. A lot of people can mistake this for simple pessimism, but it has none of the sense of passivity and futility that often come with pessimism. A determined focus on all the things that can possibly go wrong can be extremely mobilizing and galvanizing. (Would that the Bush administration had embraced *this* kind of fear in the run-up to the war in Iraq!)

To understand how this worst-case thinking can play a constructive role in an organization, let me give you what may seem like a trivial example. At Intel Israel, as at most companies, whenever my managers would propose a new strategic initiative, they would put together the inevitable slide presentation. And equally inevitably, almost like clockwork, they would delay any discussion of potential risks to the project until the very last slide—at which point, of course, we had already run out of time.

So I developed a simple rule in order to make the reality of risks to our survival very real to them. "Don't wait until the last slide to tell me about the risks," I told them. "Put a 'hand grenade' icon next to every point where there is even the least question of potential jeopardy."

People hated it. They didn't want to draw attention to where the land mines were. They assumed that by identifying potential obstacles they would ruin their chances for getting their project approved. In fact, the precise opposite turned out to be the case. The more they surfaced the key risks and uncertainties, and the more we discussed them in our management team, the more we increased our comfort level with the proposal and the more likely it became that it would be approved. The long-term result was to create an atmosphere in which people were aware of potential threats to the business but also comfortable with taking the necessary risks to meet those threats and continue to succeed.

Setting "Impossible" Goals

It's one thing to get an organization focused on survival when it faces a serious crisis; it's quite another when things seem to be going well. In such situations, one of the most effective ways to insist on survival is to set not just *stretch* goals, but *impossible* goals.

Especially in good times, when the organization doesn't seem to face any clear external threats, asking for the impossible creates a kind of "virtual" survival situation. Almost by definition, it poses the likelihood of failure; odds are that the organization will not succeed. But what often happens is that people become so engaged in doing what's necessary to meet the impossible goals that they reach levels of performance they never thought possible—thus strengthening greatly the organization's long-term prospects.

For example, when we established the Jerusalem fab in the mid-1980s, I was determined to do something that had never really been done inside Intel before: to compete on costs. At that time Intel was still a relatively young company, and the lion's share of focus had always been on innovation and product performance—not cost competitiveness. We already had a labor-cost advantage in Israel of about 15 to 20 percent compared to Intel's U.S. fabs. But I didn't want to rely on that wage differential alone. Rather, I wanted our productivity to be so good that we would be able to compete on costs with any semiconductor fab anywhere in the world. To achieve this goal, I set an "impossible" target of cutting the average cost per die of the EPROM (our first product) by roughly fourfold—from $2.50, the best performance in Intel at the time, to sixty-six cents. I christened this program "Sixty-Six Cents or Die."

To be honest, I had absolutely no idea whether we could reach this goal. But I wanted to set a dramatic target to get people focused on cost. We created a pirate flag with the campaign slogan and flew it from the flagpole in front of the fab. We came up with new metrics to track our progress—for example, complementing the traditional industry focus on "die yield" (the number of usable integrated circuits per wafer) with a new focus on what we called "line yield" (the number of usable wafers that moved through the production line during a given period of time). We collected these statistics daily and communicated the results broadly through the fab workforce. I wanted everybody to feel that if we didn't meet the goal, we would be sunk.

The campaign had an impact. Employees in the fab started to focus relentlessly on costs. They would put off purchasing new equipment until it was absolutely necessary. They reduced parts inventory significantly and improved productivity through effective and innovative debugging of new equipment. People worked so hard and were so creative in finding ways to save money and improve productivity that they did not even realize just how extraordinary their performance was.

The fact is, we never quite achieved the sixty-six cents target. But we came close. And as a result, we were able to bring the costs of the fab down so much that as Intel's microprocessor production ramped up in the late 1980s, we were able to win the lion's share of production for the 286 and subsequent generations of Intel's microprocessor product line. Because we were so focused on potential failure, we were able to survive through success.

A Catalyst for Innovation

I mentioned earlier that when I first began talking about being the last Intel operation to close in a crisis, many people at Intel Israel thought the message was too negative—especially for an innovation-driven business like semiconductors. They didn't want to just survive; they wanted to thrive! But in my experience there is a highly synergistic relationship between survival and innovation. For one thing, the imperative of continuous innovation in today's global economy is a key factor in creating the turbulence that makes long-term survival more difficult. But perhaps even more important, threats to survival can become a powerful stimulus for new innovation.

For an example of this synergy between survival and innovation, consider a threat that Intel Israel faced in the early 1990s. Typically, a semiconductor manufacturing facility has a relatively limited life, usually somewhere between ten and fifteen years. Rapid advances in chip design tend to rely on parallel advances in manufacturing and process technology. As innovation moves forward, a fab designed for one generation of technology can quickly find itself obsolete.

We faced this situation in 1993, when we began to realize that the Jerusalem fab was nearing the end of its useful life. The fab had been designed in the mid-1980s to manufacture products with channel lengths of one-and-a-half microns (a micron is one millionth of a meter). Channel length defines the distance between the two terminals (known as the *source* and the *drain*) in a transistor. It's a key metric of a chip's performance, because the shorter the channel, the more transistors can be placed on a chip, and the better the performance in terms of speed and reliability. One-and-a-half microns was adequate for Intel's 386 microprocessor, the product we were running at the time, but the new 486 had a minimum channel length of one micron. If we hoped to compete for the 486 and subsequent generations of Intel's microprocessor technology, we would have to retool the plant. Specifically, we would have to completely replace the fab's laminar-flow air-conditioning system, because the smaller the channel length, the purer the air would have to be in the fab's cleanroom.

The looming obsolescence of the Jerusalem fab was actually a quite serious threat to my vision for Intel Israel at the time. In the early '90s we had started planning to build a second, more technologically advanced fab in Jerusalem, and by 1993 we had reached agreement with the Israeli government about an incentives package for the new plant—only to be informed at the last minute by Intel corporate that they had decided to build the next fab in Arizona, not Israel. So unless we could find a way to extend the life of the original Jerusalem facility, we would lose our foothold in semiconductor manufacturing. What's more, because nobody in corporate was asking us to modernize the fab, we would have to figure out a way to do it without stopping production—not even for a single day.

My facilities people said it was impossible. A semiconductor fab's air-conditioning system is critical for continuously filtering the air of the cleanroom and making sure impurities don't get introduced into the chip-making process and ruin the semiconductors. There was no way we could build a whole new air-conditioning system while keeping the plant open. It had never been done anywhere—not at Intel or at any other semiconductor manufacturer.

I tried to explain that this wasn't a satisfactory answer. "Don't tell me why it can't be done," I said. "Tell me how we can do it and what the costs will be. I don't care how crazy the ideas are; just come up with something. Take a month and see if you can figure it out."

Three weeks later, the team returned to tell me, "We think we've found something, but you won't buy it." The basic idea was to "raise the roof" of the Jerusalem fab's cleanroom by adding a new structure on top and turning the existing roof into a false ceiling. Above this false ceiling we would install the new air-conditioning system in modules, section by section. As each new section of the system became functional, we would then break through the false ceiling and connect the new air-conditioning system to the existing one, in effect creating a hybrid system. By the end of the process we would have a completely new system, able to handle Intel's new one-micron technology. Retrofitting the entire plant would take time—about a year and a half—but it would have the advantage of allowing us to introduce the new system piece by piece without stopping the production line. The team estimated the cost of the project at about $10 million.

It wasn't the money that I was worried about. The fact is, from Intel's point of view, $10 million was a relatively small amount of money to extend the life of the fab—certainly far less than the roughly $1 billion it would have cost at the time to build a brand new fab. But could we really pull it off? Despite the risks, I took the plan to the company's senior executives, who would have to sign off on the capital expenditure. "Are you sure you can do it without affecting current production?" asked Craig Barrett, who had recently become Intel's chief operating officer. To be honest, I wasn't completely sure that the plan would work. But I told him that we had the risks under control.

It took three or four months of trial and error to figure out the best way to build the new ceiling, install each module of the new air-conditioning system, and connect it to the existing system. You can't imagine the facilities team's pride when they finally figured it out and took me to see the first successfully working module. Over the next eighteen months we proceeded step by step, installing a new module, linking it to the existing system, then moving on to the next area of the fab. The project had a galvanizing effect, not just on the facilities team but on the entire fab workforce. Because everyone was so worried that production might suffer, they went out of their way to maintain and even improve on our performance. The paradoxical result: our output was even better during and after the project than before.

This approach to modernizing a cleanroom's air-filtering system had never been done before—and I suspect it has never been done since! Yet it is an excellent example of how focusing on survival and asking the impossible can stimulate risk taking and innovation. The modernization of the Jerusalem fab was not only key to our winning a significant part of Intel's global production for the 486 microprocessor, but it also contributed to our winning the next round in the global competition for investment in Intel's expanding production facilities: the creation in 1996 of a second Intel Israel fab in the town of Qiryat Gat.

In March 2008 the Jerusalem fab finally closed down, after twenty-three years of operation (which in the fast-changing semiconductor industry must be some kind of record). Yet despite the closing of the facility, semiconductor manufacturing at Intel Israel couldn't be healthier. In 2005, Intel announced that it would build a second fab at Qiryat Gat. The $3.5 billion investment, the largest ever by a private company in Israel's history, will fund what will be one of the largest and most technologically advanced semiconductor manufacturing facilities in the world. At the new Qiryat Gat plant, channel length will be forty-five nanometers (a nanometer is one thousand-millionth of a meter), allowing transistors so small that thirty million can fit on the head of a pin.

Of course, I'm now completely retired from Intel and had nothing to do with the decision. Yet I have to believe that this investment didn't happen by coincidence. It happened because we created an organizational culture that, in good times and in bad, never took its survival for granted. It happened because we created an organization determined to be the last place to close in a crisis.

2

LEADING AGAINST
THE CURRENT

Survival requires risk taking. Taking risks often involves doing the unexpected—and sometimes the seemingly impossible—even in the face of considerable opposition. For that reason, leadership the hard way means leading against the current—for example, competing on costs at the Jerusalem fab when the rest of Intel was still focused exclusively on product innovation and performance, or replacing the fab's air-filtering system without shutting down the production line.

I believe that leading against the current is a general principle of leadership in an environment of high turbulence. In my experience, often the best thing to do in the middle of a crisis or when facing major uncertainty is precisely the *opposite* of what seems to be the safest or most commonsensical thing at the time. I don't mean to suggest that leaders should simply be contrary for contrariness's sake. But I do believe that acting against the current is an extremely effective way to turn a crisis situation inside out and reframe a threat as an opportunity.

Once again, an analogy to flying is appropriate. When a plane loses lift and goes into a free fall, the first inclination is to pull on the controls to regain altitude. But it's precisely the wrong thing to do. A plane at the beginning of a free fall has very little velocity. In that state, trying to lift the nose and pull out of the fall only slows the plane down even more, leading to a stall. Instead, the counterintuitive action a pilot needs to learn is to push *down* on the controls—in other words, to make the free fall even worse. It's the only way to acquire sufficient velocity to regain lift and come out of the dive.

Leading against the current is the equivalent of making the free fall worse. By embracing turbulence and not taking the easy way out, a leader is in a better position to jar the organization out of its collective rut. In this respect, leading against the current can be an excellent way to mobilize an organization.

To effectively lead against the current, however, a leader has to have some distinctive characteristics. First, you must be simultaneously an "insider" and an "outsider" in the organization you are leading. To do things differently, you first must be able to see things differently. Only the leader who remains something of an outsider can see around the corner of the latest crisis to perceive the potential opportunity hidden in the midst of a threat. And only from a position on the edge of the organization can the leader effectively challenge followers' conventional wisdom, instincts, and initial impulses and impressions.

Second, to lead against the current, you must be unafraid to make decisions or take actions that appear "crazy." Sometimes they may in fact *be* crazy, but more often than not they will be in response to emerging imperatives that you as the leader anticipate or sense but that the organization as a whole hasn't really perceived yet. A leader who is anticipating the next challenge will likely be marching to a different drummer, making choices that appear unorthodox and that, in the beginning at least, may be very difficult to justify—at least in the terms or logic commonly accepted in the organization.

Third, a leader against the current has to know how to manage the tension between, on the one hand, persevering in the face of opposition, and on the other, encouraging dissent and responding to it. Leading against the current means not taking "no" for an answer. You need to know how to push back—and not only "down" inside the organization, but also "across" and "up" inside the broader hierarchy of which you are a part. But being persistent in the face of opposition does not mean somehow ignoring or dismissing what others have to say—indeed, precisely the opposite. When leading against the current, it becomes all the more important to consider things from multiple points of view, especially those of people who disagree with you.

This brings me to a much-discussed—and, in my opinion, routinely misunderstood—theme of the management literature: the topic of *resistance*. So-called experts in change management are always providing advice on how leaders can "minimize resistance." I couldn't disagree more. Any against-the-current decision worth its salt will spark considerable opposition and resistance. And rather than avoiding it or minimizing it, it's far better to welcome it, seek it out, and engage with it head-on.

Indeed, I think that often the goal of the leader should be to *maximize* resistance—in the sense of encouraging disagreement and dissent, bringing resistance out into the open so it can be debated and addressed. Doing so can help you understand the fears, concerns, and perspectives of people in the organization. And in some cases, resistance and dissent can represent an important corrective when you go too far.

When an organization is in a crisis, *lack* of resistance can itself be a big problem. It can mean either that the change you are trying to create isn't radical enough—and is therefore unlikely to be truly effective—or that the opposition has gone underground, where it will be the most effective in blocking your initiative. If you aren't even aware that people in the organization disagree with you, then you are in trouble.

Encouraging and engaging with dissent also requires that you challenge your own personal inclinations. Nobody likes criticism; nobody likes to be told "you're wrong." Also, sometimes it can be difficult to differentiate between legitimate critique and mere excuses. Here's a rough rule of thumb that I've found useful: constructive critics are often very blunt; it can be extremely unpleasant to hear their point of view. Excuse-makers, by contrast, often phrase their objections in ways that seem reasonable, even innocuous—but it's just a sign that they are trying to sabotage your every move. Excuses are superficially reasonable but profoundly undermining. Genuine dissent is the opposite: it can seem unreasonable at first, but in fact often provides something that you should take into account.

But although debate, dissent, and constructive criticism are essential, it's a mistake to seek "consensus" before making a change—especially major ones affecting the fundamental direction of the organization. The more radical the change, the less possible it is to develop a consensus in advance. So let all views be heard, but in the end, it will be up to you to make the final decision. A genuine leader must always be prepared to act alone.

Leadership as Counterculture

A typical story one often hears about Israeli high-tech entrepreneurs involves a couple of guys who meet as officers in the Israeli Defense Forces (IDF), usually in some elite unit, frequently military intelligence. They forge close bonds in the army's high-pressure environment, where one's decisions as a leader can literally mean life or death. After returning to civilian life, they apply the leadership skills they acquired in the military to the challenging task of building a new business (often, one that commercializes technology first developed by the military).

It's a nice story, but that wasn't my experience. Sure, I served in the IDF in the late 1950s, but I was in anything but an elite unit. And when I had the chance to become an officer, I turned it down. After all those years in orphanages, the last thing I wanted was the regimentation of army life.

No, as strange as it may sound, the experience that probably taught me more than any other about the importance of leading against the current was my involvement in the Berkeley counterculture of the 1960s. In 1962, during my last year as an undergraduate at the Technion, Israel's equivalent to MIT, I decided that I wanted to go to the United States for graduate school. I was taking a course from an Israeli professor who had recently returned from the States, where he had become an expert in "switching theory," which was a relatively new, cutting-edge field in computer science at the time. The example of this teacher inspired me to do something similar—that is, to study in the United States and bring back a new field of technical expertise to Israel. I applied to a number of American engineering schools, including Purdue and MIT, but the University of California was the only one to offer me a stipend for my living expenses. So in the summer of 1963 I found myself flying from Tel Aviv to New York and then traveling cross-country by car to Berkeley.

It was a turbulent time. Not long after I arrived at Berkeley, John F. Kennedy was assassinated. That first year, civil rights became a burning issue on campus as scores of students were arrested at sit-ins designed to force Bay Area businesses to hire more black employees. In 1964, I witnessed the rise of the Free Speech Movement, which briefly closed the university down, as well as the first stirrings of the San Francisco Bay Area counterculture, which culminated in the Summer of Love in 1967. And throughout the period there was growing student activism against the Vietnam War. At my Ph.D. graduation ceremony in 1969, there was a massive walkout of students in protest against the war.

As a foreigner, I was fascinated by these events. After my experiences as a child during World War II and growing up in the constrained circumstances of Israel in the 1950s, the scene in Berkeley was like nothing I had ever experienced before. I was drawn to the atmosphere of freedom, creativity, and self-expression. The old '60s slogan "Do your own thing" had a powerful impact on me.

At Berkeley, I led a kind of double life. All day long, I lived in the world of engineering, going to classes, working in the lab, studying advanced topics in electronics and computer science. But then, at five o'clock, I would leave my circuits behind and enter the world of the counterculture—distributing leaflets, participating in demonstrations, attending rock concerts, experimenting with drugs, and spending long hours in the bars of Berkeley and

San Francisco discussing everything from the latest developments in Vietnam to the meaning of life. Even after I started working in Silicon Valley, first at Fairchild and then at Intel, I had as many friends in the counterculture scene as I did at work.

I'll never forget one day, walking in the Haight Ashbury, the center of the hippie movement in San Francisco. Suddenly a guy drove up in a Corvette, stopped the car, stepped out, took off his suit jacket and tie, and put on a fringed jacket and beads. In an instant, the manager had transformed himself into a hippie for the evening. Forty years later, it's easy to make fun of that image, to see this transformation as somehow fake, even self-indulgent. But that's not how I saw it at the time—or even how I see it today. Rather, I view it as a symbol of the enormous freedom and flexibility in seeing things differently, the valuable insight you can get when you radically shift your perspective, the power of being simultaneously an insider and an outsider.

In one respect, the events of the 1960s in Berkeley were uncannily familiar to me. They reminded me of the power of small groups of committed people to change history—whether it was to argue for free speech inside a university, to engage in civil disobedience in support of civil rights, or to protest, and eventually stop, a war. In this, the Berkeley activists were only the latest in the line of courageous leaders I had been exposed to—like the Van Tilborghs and other members of the minority Calvinist church in Holland who had helped save Jews during the war, or the kibbutzniks and other Zionist pioneers who had played such a central role in the founding of Israel. These groups were small minorities in the worlds they lived in. They acted against great odds, took big risks, persevered in the face of opposition and setbacks, and accomplished something significant.

What I learned at Berkeley is that unless you are prepared to see things differently and go against the current, you are unlikely to accomplish anything truly important. And to go against the current, you have to be something of an outsider, living on the edge, a member of a small but vibrant counterculture.

Apart from the Mainstream

The model of the Berkeley counterculture was in the back of my mind when I first started building Intel Israel in the 1970s and '80s. I knew, of course, that for Intel Israel to be successful, we needed to make it part of the broader Intel culture. In particular, this meant introducing key Intel practices and disciplines to the free-wheeling Israeli business culture. At the same time, however, for Intel Israel to add value to Intel, we also had to find a way to take advantage of some unique Israeli strengths. And to do that, the Intel Israel organizational culture needed to be distinctive and somewhat apart from the Intel mainstream.

It's probably wise not to put too much stock in broad cultural generalizations. Still, to understand the strengths and weaknesses of the Israeli work culture, it pays to compare it to that of the United States and Japan. In some respects, the U.S. and Israeli business cultures are similar, but they are also very different. For example, both societies are what I call "frontier" cultures. But whereas the frontier mentality in the United States focuses on the "Gold Rush"—that is, getting rich quick—the frontier mentality in Israel emphasizes survival in a hostile and extremely volatile environment. As a result, the U.S. business culture is much more individualistic; every single individual is on the lookout for his or her own opportunity. In contrast, the Israeli business culture is far more team-oriented. This team orientation can have its downside. For example, Israelis can sometimes become so team-oriented that they avoid individual accountability. But on the other hand, in my experience, they communicate, share information, and collaborate far more effectively than most American teams.

This team orientation is something that Israelis share with the Japanese. But unlike most Japanese teams, Israelis combine teamwork with a remarkable flair for improvisation and innovation. Of course, this impulse to improvise also has its downside—especially when it comes to enforcing the kind of process discipline for which the Japanese are famous. Take the example of one of Intel's most important manufacturing innovations: the "Copy Exactly" program. Developed by former CEO Craig Barrett, Copy Exactly is a system of methods and practices for training the employees in Intel's semiconductor fabs to copy exact procedures as a way to transfer new technologies from one location to another. The approach has given Intel a competitive advantage in quickly ramping up production runs for new processes and technologies.

It was extremely difficult to get Copy Exactly to take root in Israel. In the beginning, people saw it as drag on our ability to improvise—and therefore a potential threat to our competitiveness. But over time I was able to convince them that if we could somehow combine the Israeli flair for improvisation with the kind of disciplined execution represented by the Copy Exactly program, we would be in an even stronger position. Eventually we decided that whenever we came up with improvements in a particular manufacturing process, we would go to the fab that had originated it to get our "deviation" incorporated into the standard procedures. We didn't always succeed, but sometimes we did. When we were successful, the fact that we had originated the improvement meant that we had a temporary advantage over other Intel fabs. And as the new improvements rippled through the entire Intel manufacturing system, our reputation inside the company grew.

I believe that when Israeli teams harness their natural talent for innovation without sacrificing discipline, they can't be beat when it comes to solving engineering and manufacturing problems. Once, during the heyday of Japanese manufacturing, a Japanese journalist asked me which team I would prefer to lead— a Japanese team or an Israeli team. I told him that there was no question in my mind: the Israeli team, because although it is possible to instill discipline in an Israeli team, it is extremely difficult to instill creativity in a Japanese team.

When it came to Copy Exactly, we were able to find a productive point of compromise between the Israeli work culture and Intel's broader culture. But in some cases compromise wasn't possible. In those situations I was fully prepared to take tough actions to establish and maintain our autonomy so that we could leverage

Intel Israel's unique capabilities—even if it sometimes rubbed my colleagues in California the wrong way.

One of the early challenges we faced in building Intel Israel, for example, was to establish the principle inside Intel that we were a genuine center of operations, not just a "hiring hall" where Intel's U.S. operations could come to find good people. If we were constantly vulnerable to having our best people lured away to positions in the States, we would never be able to build a strong organization in Israel. In the long run that wouldn't be in the best interests of Intel Corporation.

To give that principle some teeth, I instituted a rule that to many seemed draconian: whenever people from Intel Israel went on temporary assignment to the United States (which we encouraged, mainly for training purposes), they were forbidden to transfer permanently to a U.S. unit. Rather, they had to come back to Israel, fulfill their commitments to Intel Israel, and then transfer. If they refused to do so, they had to leave Intel altogether and pay a penalty of $50,000.

Many of Intel's U.S. executives had a hard time accepting this rule. Indeed, it seemed to go against everything the company stood for. The Intel culture was a meritocracy, the kind of place where good people were given a lot of freedom. And like many large corporations, Intel *encouraged* the free transfer of employees across organizational units. It was a great way for the employees to get to know the business, build an internal network, and have exposure to different kinds of responsibilities and skills.

For all these reasons, my no-transfer rule was a source of considerable tension. "This is a free country," some of my U.S. counterparts would tell me. "How can you tell somebody what to do?" Some saw the rule as almost an act of disloyalty. "Here's this guy," they would say, "He came here for two years and now he wants to stay. That's his free choice. Would you rather that he left the company than work for us? Where's your loyalty to Intel?"

From their perspective these were perfectly reasonable questions. After all, wasn't I denying my people the opportunity to do precisely what I had done when I was in California—that is, to "do your own thing"? But I was looking at the situation differently, from the perspective of what it would take for Intel Israel to grow and develop over the long term. As I knew better than anyone, the lure of the States was just too great. If we couldn't enforce the no-transfer provision, I felt, we would never get Intel Israel off the ground.

Because I was convinced that the no-transfer rule was essential to our long-term survival, I was prepared to fight to enforce it. In one case, for example, one of my people was working in an Intel organization headed by Paul Ottelini, Intel's current CEO. At the end of his rotation, the individual informed me that he wanted to stay with the unit and that Ottelini supported him. My insistence that he return led to a confrontation that eventually went all the way to the very top of the company. At a meeting with Paul, Andy Grove (then CEO), and Craig Barrett, I explained my logic. If I couldn't enforce the no-transfer rule, Intel Israel would be reduced to a recruiting office, not a real operation. I also explained that I believed the principle was so important that I was prepared to resign if I didn't have their support. Eventually they agreed to send the guy back to Israel.

In another case, I took a position that seemed even more extreme. Remember my efforts, described in Chapter One, to prevent the layoff of our software development group in Haifa? Well, at the time, one of the software engineers on the team had just traveled on a rotation to the United States. When he heard the news that his home unit in Israel was being disbanded, he asked to stay permanently with the Intel organization that he was working with there.

This was a much tougher decision. On the one hand, the Haifa software systems group didn't really exist anymore, and the future of the team members was uncertain. Under the circumstances, it seemed unreasonable to refuse my employee's request. On the other hand, I had just convinced Intel's CEO to throw me a financial lifeline. And I knew that if I made one exception to my no-transfer rule, it would be like opening the floodgates. So I said no. The software engineer was furious—so much so that he quit in protest and joined a California software startup.

For a long time I felt that I had made a terrible mistake. Perhaps this time my impulse to go against the current had gone too far. Here one of my goals had been to save the highly talented people in the systems software unit for Intel—yet my actions had led one of the best people in the group to leave the company altogether.

Two years later, one of my direct reports approached me warily. He had gotten a call from the software engineer who had left in a huff. He now wanted to return to Intel. What did I think? My subordinate probably expected me to be angry, unwilling to even consider the idea that the software engineer might return. In fact, I was extremely pleased. I could think of no greater achievement for our organization than that even after all that had happened, he wanted to come back. Later, he went on to head the Haifa design center.

Winning the War for Talent

The no-transfer rule was just one of a whole set of against-the-current decisions that I took to build a strong organization at Intel Israel. Others involved the kind of people that I tried to attract to come to the organization in the first place. In this case I often had to push not against my colleagues in the States but against my own people.

Success in the semiconductor industry is largely a "war for talent."[1] In particular, the relative scarcity of top engineering talent has historically been a major constraint on a company's growth. The original establishment of Intel Israel in 1974 was a direct result of Intel's quest to find fresh sources of talent. The reason we created the Haifa design center in the first place was to tap in to the rich vein of technical talent in the Israeli engineering community. (Few people realize it, but Israel has an enormous reservoir of engineering talent. Today, out of every 10,000 employees in Israel there are some 135 engineers—compared with only 70 in the United States.)

Yet I was determined to find ways to expand the pool of potential hires by moving beyond what I saw as the relatively narrow focus on engineers that was typical in the industry in the United States and Israel. In the early days of the semiconductor industry it was a common assumption that to design chips (the field known as "design engineering") you had to be an engineer. I disagreed. I believed that people trained in more science-based disciplines—physicists, chemists, and the like—would make just as good chip designers as people with traditional engineering degrees. To test that intuition, when I first came back to Israel in 1974, instead of working full time for Intel I took a teaching job in a new School for Applied Science at the Hebrew University in Jerusalem (later I would become director of the school), to start building a cadre of potential future Intel Israel employees.

The expansion of Intel Israel into semiconductor manufacturing posed another recruiting challenge. By the early 1990s Intel Israel was growing so quickly and the kinds of jobs we needed to fill had broadened so much that even this expanded technical labor pool wasn't enough. I was constantly receiving messages from our recruiting organization about the difficulty of attracting good people. "We're going to have to pay more," my HR people kept telling me, "to get the people that we want." But I was worried that simply offering more money would end up attracting the kind of people that we didn't really want. I wasn't looking for individuals motivated primarily by money. I wanted people who could get excited about our vision and who wanted to make a difference. So I responded: instead of paying more money, why don't we start recruiting nontechnical people with backgrounds in the liberal arts?

This was long before the wave of "diversity" had washed over the business world. But I was convinced that we could get significantly more leverage from a more diverse workforce. My interest in employee diversity had nothing to do with any altruistic desire to make opportunities available to a wider range of people. It was purely self-interested: we needed to do something different to keep pace with Intel Israel's rapid growth.

The decision had major consequences for how we went about recruiting. For one thing, it required a wholesale transformation in our interviewing and hiring processes. But it called for an even bigger change at the level of organizational psychology. In effect, I was saying to my managers, all of whom had technical backgrounds and had been very successful within the Intel Israel organization, "Great job, now go out and start hiring people who are *not* like you!"

Many people didn't like it. Although no one put it quite this way, I suspect they felt that the new recruiting policy somehow devalued their own training, experience, and contribution. And some simply disagreed that nontechnical people could ever make it in what was, after all, a technology-driven business and company. Another complication was that, because more women were represented in the ranks of nontechnical graduates than among technical graduates, broadening our pool to include nontechnical graduates would inevitably mean hiring a lot more women into our professional and managerial ranks—not an easy step for our traditionally male-dominated high-tech culture. There was a lot of resistance—some of it due to habit, some of it deliberate. It's hard for a leopard to change its spots—especially when it is a successful leopard.

A key moment of truth for me in the campaign to broaden our labor pool came about two years after I had announced the change in hiring practices, at a point when Intel Israel was becoming well known for its supposed efforts to reach out to nontechnical candidates. I had been invited by the dean of students at Tel Aviv University to give a recruiting lecture. After the talk, she took me aside to say, "I'm very impressed with your philosophy. But I have to tell you, what you say isn't reflected in the signals we are getting from your recruiters." She went on to describe how the dominant recruiting messages coming from Intel were still all about engineering, computer science, and the like. I realized that I would need to start intervening systematically in hiring decisions to push the organization in the direction that I wanted.

In one case, for example, I learned that a woman with five children had been summarily rejected for a midlevel position in the HR department in Haifa. When I asked why, I was told "She has five kids and lives too far away. It just won't work." Not good enough, I told them, and I simply forced the center to hire her (today, she is running the HR department).

It took nearly a decade of pushing back against the organization to increase significantly nontraditional hires at Intel Israel. For example, at one point I began insisting that 50 percent of our new hires must be women. We never quite reached that goal. But because we had it as a goal, we ended up having many more women at Intel Israel than one would find at a typical Israeli company—or even in the semiconductor industry in the United States.

Eventually the pushing paid off. To give just one example: as of this writing, of the roughly thirty plant managers running Intel's seventeen semiconductor fabs around the world, only five are women—and of those five, two are in Israel. One, Maxine Fassberg, is a former high school chemistry teacher. The other, Jenny Cohen-Dorfler, is a former social worker who used to provide social services to the urban poor. They are responsible for literally millions of dollars of annual output at some of the most advanced semiconductor facilities in the world.

Learning from Mistakes

When you lead against the current, inevitably you make mistakes. The challenge is not so much avoiding these mistakes, which is impossible, as knowing how to recover from them once they are made. That's why it is important to listen to dissent. Dissent that persists or that represents a point of view for which you don't have a good answer is a signal that a course correction is necessary.

Take, for example, another against-the-current decision I made: to institute a comprehensive program of lateral transfers for senior managers inside the Intel Israel organization. Traditionally, Intel has always been a pretty functional organization. Especially in the early days, executives tended to come up either through the technology and product-development side of the business or through manufacturing (or, still later, through marketing). By the early 1990s, however, I became convinced that we needed to provide our managers with a much broader range of experiences, to cycle them through multiple functions so that they would acquire the full range of skills necessary for leading a modern business organization.

I was motivated in part by my own experience. At heart I was a researcher, and I had grown up on the research side of Intel. But when we set up the Jerusalem fab, I had had to go back to square one and learn how to run a highly demanding manufacturing operation. My capabilities as a leader grew by orders of magnitude as a result. I felt that a system of lateral transfers would greatly increase the flexibility of our management team. I also believed it would pay organizational dividends as well. Someone who was a relative outsider, I reasoned, would bring a fresh perspective, not take things for granted, ask hard questions, and discover new and better ways of doing things. The ultimate result would be a step-function improvement in performance.

To kick off the lateral-transfer program and break through the traditional assumptions of the Intel Israel culture, I decided to do something dramatic. I announced that the heads of the Haifa design center and the Jerusalem fab would switch jobs.

The manager who moved from the design center to the fab was an extremely cautious and careful manager. He spent the first three months in his new role simply trying to understand how the fab worked. Only when he had his feet on the ground did he start making any changes. As a result, his transition went smoothly. And as I anticipated, there were major benefits in operational improvement.

The former manufacturing manager who went from Jerusalem to Haifa, however, was another story. On paper, he was a logical leader for the design center. He had a strong background in engineering, and one of our strategic goals at the time was to introduce more process discipline to the innovative but sometimes disorganized practices of the center. However, unlike his counterpart, he started making big changes right away, which sparked a strong negative counter-reaction. Soon I began hearing criticism about his management style—not only from center employees but also from the executives in California running Intel's global Microprocessor Group, of which the Haifa center was a part. "You need to bring in someone who knows how to run a design center," they told me.

At first I ignored the criticisms. I thought they were the typical response of an inbred culture that didn't want to try new ways of doing things. I was committed to the principle of lateral transfers. And I was the last person to back down in the face of criticism or resistance.

But eventually the backlash caused me to realize that I had made a big mistake. I had underestimated the clash between the manufacturing culture and the design culture. I had also underestimated the amount of learning that would be required and the amount of support that at least some of the people placed in unfamiliar roles would therefore need. Eventually I came to the conclusion that the design center's new manager just wasn't going to make it; his relationship with his peers and employees had deteriorated to the point that he could never be successful in the role. Reluctantly, I replaced him with someone who had come up through the ranks of Intel's design organization.

Another thing I underestimated was the human price of failure. I had taken an extremely successful manufacturing manager and put him in a situation where he failed. As a result, there was no real place left for him in the organization, so he decided to leave. I felt responsible for the loss of a good manager. The failure wasn't just his; it was mine.

The failure, however, didn't cause me to give up on my lateral-transfer plan. Instead, I started stressing the important cultural dimension of the change. "Take time to learn the culture," I advised managers moving into new and unfamiliar roles. I also began to place more emphasis on the need for senior managers like myself to provide ongoing support to help people make the transition.

Today, lateral transfers of this type are routine at Intel Israel. And the diversity of experience that managers pick up over the course of their careers has put them in a good position to succeed, not just at Intel Israel but in Intel worldwide. For example, Alexander Kornhauser, the manager who fifteen years ago successfully made the transition from the design center to the Jerusalem fab, went on to manage the construction and startup of Intel Israel's first fab in Qiryat Gat. He was my successor as general manager of Intel Israel and, until recently, head of Intel's global flash-memory manufacturing group.

From the Periphery to the Center

Every one of these against-the-current actions was designed to make Intel Israel a distinctive counterculture, with a strong local identity and esprit de corps. Paradoxically, this powerful local culture with its inclination to act against the current is precisely what has allowed the organization to become an integral part of Intel worldwide today.

Recent events dramatically demonstrate just how deeply leading against the current has been institutionalized in the Intel Israel culture. In the summer of 2006, Intel introduced a new generation of microprocessor technology, known as Core 2 Duo, that Intel CEO Paul Ottelini has called "a revolutionary leap" compared to Intel's earlier microprocessors.[2] The technology was created at the Haifa design center—and the way in which it was developed is a classic example of against-the-current leadership.

Traditionally, Intel's microprocessors were optimized for speed. The company had always promoted faster clock speed—the rate at which a chip executes instructions—as the most important criterion for microprocessor performance. But increased speed meant higher power consumption and increased heat. A high-performing microprocessor could generate as much heat as a small television set.

The Intel Israel designers in Haifa who were charged with creating a microprocessor for the laptop market decided to take a different approach. They realized that unless they could design a microprocessor that consumed less power and produced less heat, they would never be able to create ultrathin laptops. The fan would have to be thicker than the laptop itself. So instead of optimizing processor speed, they optimized low power consumption (which minimized heat).

At the time, the project was so outside the Intel mainstream that at one point it was actually cancelled. But Intel Israel designers didn't take no for an answer. And as the laptop market grew and became more important to the company as a whole, having a low-power, low-heat microprocessor proved to be a distinct advantage. An early version of Intel Israel's new microprocessor eventually became a key component in Intel's Centrino package, which hit the market in March 2003 and was the catalyst for three years of 13-percent annual sales growth at Intel from 2003 to 2005.

Today, Intel Israel is the global headquarters of the company's all-important mobile computing platform, which is run by an Israeli senior vice president, Dadi Perlmutter. What's more, the core competence that the Haifa design center developed—microprocessors that combine high performance with relatively low power consumption—is turning out to be critical for other key Intel markets, such as servers and home entertainment, as well. So much so that today Intel's global microprocessor design group is run out of Haifa.

You might say that by leading against the current, we succeeded in injecting Intel Israel directly into the Intel mainstream.

3

LEVERAGING RANDOM OPPORTUNITIES

Increased turbulence has a complex impact on the nature of opportunity. Put simply, the more turbulent the environment, the more random opportunities become—and the more difficult it is to identify and take advantage of them. Rapid change, sudden disruptions, and high uncertainty all throw up unanticipated threats, but also unforeseen possibilities. Sometimes the greatest opportunity lies in the middle of the most threatening crisis, so it can be hard to distinguish the one from the other. The challenge of the leader is to seek out such random opportunities and leverage them for the success and survival of the organization.

When most managers think about pursuing opportunities, they usually do so in the context of strategic planning. That's precisely not what I am talking about here. In fact, leveraging random opportunities is the antithesis of strategic planning. It has a different logic and requires different skills. Most large established organizations are not very good at it.

Don't get me wrong; I know that planning is important. Any complex organization needs to have a plan. But no plan, no matter how detailed, is really equal to the complexity and richness of possibility thrown up by turbulence. The more turbulent a company's situation, the more difficult it is to develop a detailed strategic plan in advance and then execute it. The environment is too uncertain; conditions change too rapidly and in unanticipated ways. Once you enter the eye of the thunderstorm, most plans get thrown out the window (we'll see a detailed example of this phenomenon in the next chapter). If you become too wedded to your plan, you run the risk of losing your ability to adapt to new circumstances.

In the end, improvisation is just as important as planning—and perhaps even more important. I'm even tempted to say that while managers plan, leaders seek out and exploit random opportunities.

Leveraging random opportunities isn't a linear or systematic process. It's not analytical—or at least not in the usual way that term is understood. It is more akin to intuition; though it has a logic all its own, that logic is rarely self-evident. To identify random opportunities requires openness, awareness, and an ability to see connections that at first glance don't appear to be there. It's as much a state of mind as a way of behaving or acting.

Take, for example, the modernization of the Jerusalem fab described in Chapter One. In that situation, I faced a problem—the looming obsolescence of the fab—which produced a conviction that "something needs to be done." I didn't have a plan. The fact is, I had no idea what exactly we should do. I just knew we needed to do something. But that imperative to do something (in order to survive) became the catalyst for improvisation, an innovative search for a solution. The result: the highly creative approach of raising the roof of the cleanroom and incrementally modernizing the laminar-flow air-filtering system without stopping production.

As this example suggests, leveraging random opportunity means two things: first, reframing a problem or crisis as a potential opportunity, and second, seizing the moment and committing to act without necessarily having a clear plan of what you are going to do.

In my experience, the capacity to identify and exploit random opportunities is relatively rare in big organizations. That makes sense when you think about it. Bureaucracy is about standardization, establishing routines and then executing them over and over again. Being good at recognizing random opportunities, in contrast, requires improvisation—breaking routines to take advantage of an unexpected opportunity.

So how do leaders improve their ability to spot random opportunities and take advantage of them? Four practices are especially important: having a long-term vision, staying true to your passion, seeing the opportunity at the center of every problem, and managing the delicate balance between "holding your fire" (waiting for a situation to mature) and "striking when the iron is hot" (moving quickly to take advantage of new developments). In this chapter, I'll describe some of the experiences that taught me the importance of random opportunity. And I will finally tell the story of how we created Intel Israel in the first place. It's a great example of the randomness of opportunity and the long and circuitous route a leader often has to take in order to realize his vision.

Turning a Problem Into a Product

Sometimes I think that random opportunities are the story of my life. Take, for example, the decision that was made for me, to leave the Van Tilborghs and go into a Jewish orphanage, even though I didn't really want to go. I often wonder: what would have happened if I had stayed? As a member of a rural family, I probably wouldn't have gone very far in terms of schooling. Who knows, maybe I would have become a farmer. At a minimum, I would have had a very different life—more relaxing perhaps, but certainly less eventful—than the one I eventually led.

So too with going to graduate school at Berkeley. I had no idea that this would put me within striking distance of Silicon Valley precisely at the moment when the semiconductor industry was about to take off. Would I have achieved as much as I have if I had chosen to study at, say, Purdue? Who knows?

But the experience that probably more than any other taught me the power of random opportunity was the one that led to the most significant technical achievement of my career: my invention of the EPROM in the early 1970s. That discovery has been described as a case study in turning "an intractable technical problem into a new product."[1] I see it as a classic example of taking advantage of a random opportunity. Understanding why requires going a bit into the technical details of the early semiconductor industry—so I ask my nontechnical readers to bear with me.

When I first started at Intel in 1969, there were essentially two types of semiconductor memories. Random-access memory (RAM) chips were easy to program, but a chip would lose its charge (and therefore, the information encoded on the chip) when its power source was turned off. In industry parlance, RAM chips were *volatile*.

Read-only memory (ROM) chips, by contrast, were *nonvolatile*—that is, the information encoded in the chip was fixed and unchangeable. But the process for programming ROM memories was time-consuming and cumbersome. Typically, the data had to be "burned in" at the factory: physically embedded on the chip through a process called "masking" that generally took weeks to complete. And once programmed, a ROM chip could not be easily changed.

Not long after joining Intel, I got pulled into troubleshooting a serious problem that threatened the release of the company's first semiconductor memory product, an early RAM chip known as the 1101. The chip worked fine at room temperature. But under conditions of high temperature and high humidity (the standard test, known as "85–85," consisted of running the chip at 85 degrees centigrade and 85 percent humidity), it became unstable, causing the information encoded on the chip to be lost. My assignment was to figure out what was causing this major product flaw and fix it.

A metal-oxide semiconductor (MOS) is a highly complex physicochemical device, but for the sake of simplicity we can think of it as a stack made up of four distinct layers. At the very bottom is a substrate of semiconducting material, usually silicon. As the name suggests, semiconductors such as silicon have an electrical conductivity in between that of a metal and an insulator. Because it is relatively easy to modify their conductivity, they are a key component of any semiconducting device.

On top of the semiconducting substrate is deposited a nonconducting insulator (for example, silicon dioxide), known as the *active insulator*. The layer on top of the insulator is known as a *gate* (in the 1101, it was made of polysilicon). Finally, another layer of insulator is put down on top of the gate, and metal lines are embedded in the insulator to connect the gate to the source of a voltage coming from outside the semiconductor.

When a voltage is applied to the gate, it generates an electric field that penetrates the active insulator and modifies the conductivity of the semiconducting layer, making it possible to control the current flow between the source and drain of a transistor. This creates a basic transistor switch, which is the building block of the logic gates found in an integrated circuit. It is the voltage applied to the gates of the circuit that determines whether each switch in a semiconductor is either on or off.

After a few weeks of testing, I developed a hypothesis of what was going wrong in the 1101. The heat and humidity were changing the chemical composition at the interface between the top-layer insulator and the gate, causing the chip's electric charge to migrate uncontrollably and thus changing the information in the chip's memory cells.

To test my hypothesis, I was able to take advantage of another problem with the 1101 that was totally unrelated to the one that I was troubleshooting. It turned out that due to problems in the chip fabrication process, the metal lines connected to the gates on some of the 1101 chips were breaking when they were laid down on the chip. This ruined these chips, because the metal lines could no longer carry a current to the gates and thus to all the memory cells on the device. But when I applied a voltage to these flawed chips under the high-temperature and high-humidity conditions of the 85–85 test, I was able to show that the isolated gates were in fact conducting charges, even though they were disconnected from the source of the current—proof positive that the charge was migrating along the interface of the insulator.

Once I demonstrated that charge migration was the source of the problem, the solution was relatively straightforward. By modifying the chemical composition of the insulator layer above the gate, we were able to make the interfaces more inert, thus preventing them from conducting a charge even when the temperature and humidity around the device were high.

But for some reason the anomalous image of the isolated gates that, nevertheless, still conducted charges remained fixed in my mind. No one knows when the precise moment of inspiration comes. But at a certain point I began to realize that if you intentionally designed a series of disconnected gates to "float" on top of an active insulator and then found a way to get a charge onto these "floating gates," the charge would have nowhere to go. The result would be a whole new kind of semiconductor memory, one that you could program easily (like a RAM) but that would retain its information, even in the absence of continuous power (like a ROM).

This initial concept of the floating gate, combined with a technique for charging the gates that came to be known as "avalanche injection" and a technique for erasing them using ultraviolet light, eventually led to the development of the EPROM—a nonvolatile but easily reprogrammable semiconductor memory. It was the catalyst for a whole line of innovation and development that eventually led to today's ubiquitous flash memory technology.

The EPROM had an enormous impact on Intel as a company—and on the evolution of computing. At first, we had no idea what to do with this new kind of memory, but it soon became apparent that the EPROM was the perfect twin to another new Intel product developed at the time: the programmable microprocessor. Every application using a microprocessor required read-only memory to store the program that drove the processor. With the EPROM, engineers could cut the prototyping cycle for new computer products from months literally to hours, because whenever they had to make changes to the master program, they could immediately reprogram the EPROMs that stored it.

At first we assumed that once customers had finalized a program for a new microprocessor application, they would then switch to the much cheaper ROMs in the final product. But to our surprise—and delight—we discovered that once customers got used to the instant gratification of the EPROM, they didn't want to go back. They preferred the flexibility of the more expensive EPROM even in the final product, because it allowed them to make changes up to the last minute and, over time, to easily incorporate new upgrades to the microprocessor program.

As a result, the EPROM became a cash cow that contributed tens of millions of dollars to Intel's bottom line. According to one estimate, Intel's revenues grew sevenfold, from $9 million in 1971 to $66 million in 1973, largely due to sales of the EPROM.[2] Well into the 1980s, the EPROM remained one of Intel's most profitable products. All of this was because of a new kind of semiconductor memory that I discovered almost by accident.

The experience of inventing the EPROM taught me that opportunities will emerge when you least expect them—if you have the imagination to see them.

Staying True to a Vision

Leveraging random opportunities may be the antithesis of traditional planning. It does, however, require having a long-term vision. This may seem paradoxical. If opportunity is increasingly random, wouldn't long-term vision matter less? Isn't the imperative to focus on the moment in order to adapt continually to new realities?

It's not that simple. In a fast-changing environment, you need to have a vision to be able to recognize those opportunities that really matter. A long-term vision provides the orienting framework that allows you to identify what is a genuine opportunity and what is not. Otherwise, a leader risks getting fixated on short-term perturbations in the environment and becoming trapped in an unproductive round of constantly firefighting the problem of the moment. Only when you have a long-term vision can you appropriately adapt to short-term changes and recognize the unanticipated opportunities created by a turbulent environment.

Let me give an example of how this relationship between a long-term vision and random opportunities worked in my own case. The origins of my vision for Intel Israel go all the way back to that class on switching theory at the Technion. It was then, inspired by my teacher's experience, that I got the idea to go to the United States to bring a new field back to Israel. At the time I had absolutely no idea either of what I wanted to bring back or how to do it—but I had the example of my professor and the desire to do something similar.

Once I found myself in on the ground floor of the semiconductor business, I began to think about perhaps building some kind of semiconductor research operation in Israel. Even when I was working at Fairchild, before I had completed my Ph.D., I would occasionally float the idea with my colleagues and bosses about "possibly doing something in Israel." But at the time it was just a pipe dream, not a practical possibility. Once I had invented the EPROM, I began to have the credibility inside Intel to push my vision more aggressively. But in those early years I also realized that the time was not yet ripe. Intel was still an extremely young company. It just wasn't ready to set up an operation halfway around the world.

In a turbulent environment leaders need to act quickly. Yet sometimes if you rush to make things happen, you can end up undermining your ability to recognize an unanticipated random opportunity as it emerges. It's important to realize that there are periods in the evolution of a vision when you just can't force things. It's better to sit back, bide your time, and wait for the right opportunity to take shape.

That's why in the spring of 1971, not long after I had presented the EPROM concept at a major industry conference and we had built some of the first prototype products, I decided to leave Intel for a time, to teach electrical engineering at the University of Kumasi in Ghana in West Africa. I was newly married, and my wife and I had always wanted to travel. "Do your own thing" was still my mantra. I was looking for adventure, something different, an experience of personal freedom and self-development. The EPROM concept was proven, so it seemed like a good time to leave.

People at Intel were astounded by my decision. Precisely at the moment when I had made my reputation at the company,

I was leaving. What's more, Intel had just had its first profitable year and was about to go public. To leave meant walking away from considerable stock options that would likely result in a great deal of money. But perhaps most important, although the basic concept of the EPROM had been demonstrated, the product was still very much in development. Many technical challenges had still to be solved in order to reliably manufacture the new chip. How could I possibly leave at a time like this?

I remember well a lunch I had with Andy Grove in the days before I left. He knew he couldn't convince me to change my mind. Nevertheless, he told me a story about two engineers whom he termed "Engineer A" and "Engineer B." Engineer A was the type of person who had a passion for discovery but who, once the basic concept had been proven, more or less lost interest in subsequent developments. Engineer B, by contrast, not only made great discoveries but also did the hard work of seeing the discovery through production into a great product. It was pretty clear from Andy's account which engineer he thought I was—and which created more value for a startup company like Intel.

In retrospect, I realize that Andy was trying to tell me that my decision to leave at this delicate moment was a failure of leadership. In one respect, he was absolutely right. At the time, I really was an Engineer A. My attitude was that with the demonstration of the EPROM concept, the heavy lifting had been done. Creating a manufacturing process that could reliably produce the chip was just a detail, something that could be safely left to others. No doubt I completely underestimated just how complex and difficult a challenge that would be.

But in another respect, my decision wasn't so much a failure of leadership as a fundamental choice about how and where I wanted to lead. Any successful person will invariably have access to more opportunities than he or she can ever take advantage of. Sooner or later, you have to decide what your ultimate passion is, where you really want to put your energy. Otherwise, you run the risk of being consumed by detours that don't really get you where you want to go.

For Andy, the focus of his passion was clear: building Intel into a great company. At the time he was completely preoccupied with the challenge of turning great technical ideas into profitable products. But I had a different perspective. For me, the task of building Intel certainly was important—but only if, over time, it could be a vehicle for me to create something in Israel. Although I had adjusted quite well to U.S. culture, I wanted to get back to my friends and social networks in Israel. Even more important, I was convinced that my opportunity to have an impact and make a contribution was far greater in Israel than in the United States. In 1971 I knew that the company really wasn't ready to take that step. And I worried that if I devoted myself to the EPROM, I might go down the path of a U.S. management career and that would take me too far away from my vision. So I felt the timing was right to walk away. In a sense, my decision to spend a year in Africa was a kind of compromise, a way to detach myself from Silicon Valley and California, even though I wasn't quite ready to go back to Israel.

I spent fifteen months in Africa, teaching in Kumasi and traveling throughout the continent. I suppose one could say that my time there was a kind of detour. I was biding my time until conditions were right for returning to Israel. But whatever my adventure in Africa represented to me at the time, the fact is I learned things in Africa that proved incredibly useful in ultimately realizing my vision—although, once again, there was absolutely no way to know or predict that in advance.

For example, one of the things that greatly impressed me about African culture was its rich complexity—in particular, the way many of the Africans I met seemed to balance comfortably multiple identities. Kumasi is the capital of the Ashanti people, one of the key ethnic groups in Ghana, and it wasn't unusual to meet people who took great pride in their Ashanti heritage without feeling any less Ghanaian. And given the pan-Africanist ideology of Ghana's founding president Kwame Nkrumah, many also took pride in their African identity as well.

This experience had a big impact on my thinking about the kind of organization I wanted to create when I returned to Israel. I slowly began to realize that I wanted to build a culture that reflected the best features of Intel's corporate culture but also leveraged the unique aspects of the Israeli "tribe"! By the time I left Africa, I knew that I was ready to go back to Israel, for the first time in nearly a decade.

Striking When the Iron Is Hot

If leveraging random opportunities sometimes means biding your time, it also means moving quickly and striking when the iron is hot. For me, that moment came in early 1973, when my wife and I returned to California from Africa. My plan was to work at Intel for six months or so in preparation to finally return to Israel. But as it still wasn't clear whether I could convince Intel to start an operation there, I made arrangements to teach at a new school for applied sciences at the Hebrew University in Jerusalem.

Once I returned to Silicon Valley, however, I kept hearing about a severe engineering shortage in the semiconductor industry. Perhaps the time was right to make my move. Immediately, I went to Intel's senior management team to suggest that we open a small design center in Israel. There wasn't a lot of discussion or analysis of the idea. Grove, who was Intel's COO at the time, simply organized a small group—including board chairman and leading venture capitalist Arthur Rock, head of engineering Les Vadasz, and myself—to travel to Israel to look for potential candidates. Our trip had to be postponed because of the October 1973 Yom Kippur War, and I returned to Israel by myself in January, but the group eventually came to Israel in April 1974 and hired the first five employees of the Haifa design center.

It would have been logical for me to head the Haifa operation. Nevertheless, I elected to continue at Hebrew University and work with Intel as a consultant. I felt that I could serve my long-term vision better by building a cadre of trained scientists that would be future Intel employees. I also thought the new center would have a better chance of being integrated into the company if its first manager were an American. And to be honest, I had my eyes on an even bigger prize. I knew the real action in the semiconductor industry was not in just chip design and product development but in manufacturing. I wanted Intel Israel to have a semiconductor fab.

Getting Intel comfortable with the idea of setting up a modest design center was one thing. Convincing the company to invest in the establishment of a semiconductor fab was a challenge that was orders of magnitude more difficult. Not only was it a major financial investment—at the time, a typical fab cost in the neighborhood of $150 million (today the investment is around $3.5 billion). It would also be the first time that Intel built a fab outside the United States—and at a time when it was becoming increasingly clear inside the company that manufacturing quality and reliability were essential to Intel's future. So once again I waited for the moment when the time was ripe.

A key random opportunity emerged in 1978, when I learned that Intel founder and then-CEO Gordon Moore was planning a study trip to Israel. I knew that among the many factors the company considered when choosing a site for a semiconductor fab, by far the most important was the quality of the labor force available. So when Moore came to Israel for his visit, I didn't try to sell him on the idea that Intel should build a manufacturing facility in Israel. Indeed, I didn't even bring it up. Instead, I organized a trip that would impress him with the overall capabilities of the Israeli scientific and technical community.

In those days, whenever an Intel senior executive took a study trip of this sort, he wrote a detailed report for his colleagues. I'm not a particularly careful reader of memos. But I pored over Moore's trip report like it was a commentary from the Talmud. Moore was not a highly demonstrative person; he was taciturn, a man of few words. Yet I could tell, reading between the lines, that he had been impressed with what he had seen. Within days, I was on a plane to California to start lobbying COO

Andy Grove for a manufacturing facility. Without making any commitments, Grove gave me the go-ahead to start preliminary negotiations with the Israeli government.

A critical part of the equation was convincing the government to offer a package of investment incentives and tax breaks that would make Israel competitive with other potential sites in the United States or Europe. This was standard practice in the semi-conductor industry, but it was especially important for Israel, given the relatively high level of geopolitical instability in the region. Fortunately, the two senior civil servants in Israel's Ministry of Industry and Ministry of Finance who were my primary counter-parts in the negotiations well understood the potential leverage for the economy of a major investment by Intel. But there was consid-erable public and political opposition to the incentive package.

Like many countries in the developing world, Israel had a relatively standard formula for attracting foreign investment in high-technology industries. Israeli law specified that for certain advanced, high-tech sectors, the government would provide a grant of up to 38 percent of the total amount invested. But the overall size of the total investment in this project—$150 million—was the largest ever in the country's history, which made the government subsidy a relatively large number as well: nearly $60 million.

This number provoked a lot of opposition. Two related argu-ments loomed large. First, the local electronics industry thought it was unfair that so large a subsidy was going to a foreign company. Why not support local firms instead? What's more, some critics argued that instead of subsidizing investment by a large global cor-poration, it would be better to spread the money among some of the smaller high-tech startups that were just beginning to emerge in Israel.

My position was that any deal had to be good for Israel and good for Intel, in that order. The prejudice against Intel as a foreign company was something we had encountered even when we estab-lished the Haifa design center (when there was no question of government subsidy). People had grumbled then about "a foreign corporation taking our elite manpower." Now they complained about subsidizing a foreign company that would "take all its profits out of Israel." I felt that such attitudes were a vestige of an old-fashioned economic nationalism that was completely out of place in an increasingly global economy. My attitude was, either Israel is going to be a player in the global economy or it's not. If it is, it needs to intelligently leverage investment by global companies. We had the talent to compete on the world stage. Why not take advantage of it?

As for the startup argument, I felt that it was critical for Israeli high tech to have at least a few "anchor tenants"—that is, a critical mass of large established global corporations that would help stabilize and develop the infrastructure of the high-tech sector. After all, the success rate of new startups is typically in the neighborhood of 1 to 5 percent. For the government to focus its investment subsidies exclusively on startups was just too risky and would result in a much lower return on investment.

Throughout the negotiation process, of course, I worked hard to find the leverage points of opportunity in the situation to create the best deal for Intel that I could. For example, early in our discussions I proposed that we locate the new fab in an industrial park in Jerusalem. Most people thought it was an odd decision. The logical choice would have been Haifa, where we already had our design center, or the Tel Aviv metropolitan area, which was becoming something of a center for businesses in the electronics and computing industries. Unlike these cities, Jerusalem had very little industrial infrastructure at the time.

But I understood that the very *absence* of an existing infrastructure would be an advantage. First, it would cause the Israeli government to award the maximum in tax breaks and other incentives to win the plant—which would make us all the more competitive in the internal competition against other potential sites in the United States and Europe. Second, the very fact that there was little industry in the city meant that we would have more influence in determining prevailing wage rates and more luck in recruiting employees with minimal experience in Israel's powerful and, from the perspective of a global high-tech industry, too-rigid labor unions.

After a series of tough negotiations, I finally had a government-approved incentives package that I thought was competitive. But I still had to convince Intel to build the plant. Grove declared that there would be a "bake-off," a competition between the Israeli proposal and some alternative site. He chose an Intel executive who was Irish to develop a competing proposal for building a new fab in Ireland.

The bake-off took place in a large Intel conference room before the company's senior executives. As I made our presentation, I felt confident. The competing proposal had an assigned champion, not a real one. As I moved through my presentation, I felt the energy in the room shift in my direction.

Then, near the end of my presentation, Grove asked suddenly, "What about training?" He meant, how were we going to train our brand-new workforce to start up and run the new fab? No problem, I explained. We would send the initial workforce of some 150 to 200 people to the States to work in Intel fabs there. Once trained, they would return to Israel and train the rest of the staff. Grove hit the roof. "Absolutely not!" he answered. "Do you have any idea how much it will cost to bring all those people to the States and train them? And it will be a major drag on the productivity of the U.S. fabs." With that, the meeting ended. I didn't even get the chance to finish my presentation. After all our effort, the plan seemed dead.

I was completely unprepared for Grove's response. It had never occurred to me that the training issue would be a deal-breaker. By this point, however, I knew Grove pretty well. In particular, I knew that the Andy in public was different from the Andy in private. I immediately followed him down to his office and caught up with him just before he was leaving to go skiing for the weekend. "You need to give me one more chance," I said. We scheduled another meeting for the following week.

All weekend long, I worked with the training staff to see if we could find a solution to the high costs of the training program. After analyzing the data and talking with some of the heads of other Intel fabs, we came to a new insight. Yes, the impact on fab productivity of training the Israeli workforce would be negative in the near term. But over time, as they learned how to run a fab, their presence would begin to be a major benefit. By the end of the six-month training period, they would even be contributing to the productivity of the U.S. fabs. We created a graph showing how the impact of the trainees would over time contribute to the U.S. fabs. It was that graph that clinched it when I met with Grove the following week.

The groundbreaking for the Jerusalem fab took place in July 1981. Jerusalem mayor Teddy Kolleck was there, as were the two civil servants who had led the negotiations for the Israeli government, but that was it as far as the politicians were concerned. To be honest, I think there was still a lot of skepticism that we could pull this complex project off. Some of that skepticism was warranted. This was the first time that Intel had ever built a fab outside the United States. It was the biggest construction project in the history of Israel up to that time. And we had an entire new workforce to train. It took roughly three and half years to complete the project. The fab finally opened for business in May 1985 and began running—appropriately, but coincidentally—the latest version of Intel's EPROM chip.

The establishment of the Jerusalem fab also represented a major step in my own career. Not long after approving the deal, Grove pulled me aside to say, "Dov, the design center is one thing, but manufacturing is a much bigger deal. You're going to have to run it." So I stepped down as director of the applied science school at Hebrew University to rejoin Intel as the Jerusalem fab manager and general manager for Intel Israel. My evolution into the leader of Intel Israel was complete. But my education as a leader had just begun.

Going Through the Window

Success always appears inevitable in retrospect. But at any number of points in this long multiyear process, things could have gone wrong. Indeed, occasionally they did. For example, a few years later, in 1993, we negotiated a new package with the Israeli government to expand the Jerusalem fab—only to see the deal fall through when, at the last minute, Intel decided to build its next fab in Arizona, not Israel. (It was that decision that forced us to modernize the original fab.) But we stayed flexible, all the while not taking no for an answer, and we won the next round in 1995 when we got the go-ahead to build a second Israeli fab, this time in the town of Qiryat Gat, in southern Israel near the Negev Desert.

When we established the Qiryat Gat fab, I had to go through the same political fight as I had when we were negotiating for the Jerusalem site. There were the same critiques and the same opposition—only this time, because the investment (and therefore the amount of government subsidy) was so much bigger and the process was so much more public, it was an even tougher conflict. But in the end we won. And Qiryat Gat is where Intel is building its third Israeli fab today.

Andy Grove used to say, "The thing about Dov, if he can't come through the front door, he goes through the window." It's true. I don't take no for an answer. I'm always trying to find that opportunity in the middle of whatever the problem or challenge or crisis of the moment may be—and take advantage of it. Effective leaders are good at finding random opportunities—and then exploiting them.

4

LEADERSHIP UNDER FIRE

Sooner or later, every leader faces a moment of truth—a crisis or challenge that tests his or her leadership ability to the utmost. For me, that moment of truth came in 1991 when I had to guide Intel Israel through the crisis of the First Gulf War and the Scud missile attacks of Saddam Hussein's Iraq on Israel. In the days before the start of the war, I had to make a critical decision with potentially life-threatening consequences for our employees: whether to keep our operations open, despite the threat of the missile attacks, or to close down until the crisis had passed.

Of course, many businesses remain open during wartime. But in the days before the First Gulf War, Israel confronted what appeared at the time to be an unprecedented threat. The Israeli military assumed that Iraqi missiles would be carrying chemical weapons. The government distributed gas masks and ordered every household to prepare a special sealed room in case of chemical attack. Most serious from a business perspective, in anticipation of the missile attacks the Israeli civil defense authority instructed all nonessential businesses to close and their employees to remain at home. The radical uncertainty of the situation—not knowing how many missiles would fall, where they would fall, what kind of destruction they would inflict—threatened to bring our business to a halt, even before a single missile had been launched.

It would have been easy to follow the civil defense instruction and close down. Everyone was doing it. Intel's senior executives in California would have understood. Many of our employees would probably have appreciated the opportunity to focus on preparing their families for the attacks. Yet I chose to ignore the government directive, keep our operations open, and ask our employees to continue to come to work.

Some people thought I was being irresponsible. What right did I have to risk people's lives in time of war? Others thought I was crazy. What if any of our employees were killed? What if the government took legal action? What if disgruntled employees went to the press?

Despite these risks, I stuck to my decision because I was convinced that shutting down our operations was a direct threat to the long-term survival of Intel Israel. And Intel's employees responded. In the first days of the Scud attacks, when businesses throughout the nation were closed, roughly 80 percent of Intel's employees showed up for work, day in and day out, day and night shifts included. Thanks to their heroic performance, Intel Israel was one of the few businesses in Israel (and our Jerusalem semiconductor fab the only manufacturing operation) to remain open throughout the entire six weeks of the war. Not only did we keep our commitments to global Intel, but we also established the reputation that, over time, would allow us to grow Intel Israel into an important center of excellence for the corporation.

The story of our actions during the First Gulf War is a dramatic example of the challenges to leadership in an environment of extreme turbulence. Believe me, you don't really know what turbulence means until you have had to run a business during a war! The experience taught me a lot of lessons: about the limits of even the best-laid plans, the impossibility of anticipating risks, the imperative of radical improvisation, the necessity of trusting your instincts.

But even more important, the story also effectively illustrates the three key principles of leadership the hard way described in previous chapters. Because I was so focused on our survival and continuously wary about potential threats to it, I was able to recognize that whatever else the Scud attacks represented, they were also a potential threat to the long-term viability of our business. Because I was committed to leading against the current, I was able to make the unconventional decision to stay open—despite the many risks involved and despite the fact that most businesses in Israel were taking the prudent route and shutting down. And although it may sound unfeeling, because I was always on the lookout for random opportunities, I understood intuitively that the First Gulf War was not only a threat but also an important opportunity. If we could meet our commitments despite the Scud attacks, we could establish Intel Israel's reputation in the company for years to come.

A Different Kind of War

By the early 1990s, Intel Israel had grown from a small outpost of chip designers to become a major part of Intel's burgeoning global production system. In 1986, not long after the introduction of the 386 microprocessor, Intel's senior executives had made a critical strategic decision: instead of licensing the 386 design to another semiconductor company in order to provide customers with a second-source supplier (a common practice in the semiconductor industry at the time), Intel would be the sole supplier of the product. This gave the company the potential to maintain a highly profitable monopoly on supply of the 386—but it also put intense pressure on Intel's fabs to keep up with soaring demand.

By the early 1990s, our Jerusalem fab, Intel's first outside the United States, was a key player in executing this single-source strategy. We were responsible for about three-quarters of the global output of the 386 and were gearing up to compete inside Intel for production of the new, more advanced 486 chip. We were operating seven days a week and running two twelve-hour shifts in order to keep up with customer demand. Meanwhile, our design center in Haifa was hard at work on developing new products that would be critical to Intel's future, including key components of what would become the next-generation Pentium microprocessor.

When Iraq invaded Kuwait in August 1990, I knew that war was likely. So I appointed a task force of senior managers to develop a contingency plan in case Israel was drawn into the conflict. At the time, we were assuming it would be a conventional war, and we were confident that we could handle it. We had had experience with what war would mean for our business from the call-up of reservists during Israel's incursion into Lebanon in 1982. We had contingencies for replacing key personnel who were called up to the military, for operating the plant on a skeleton crew, and for scaling back the private transportation service we used to bring our employees to work at the Jerusalem fab (a typical arrangement at most large Israeli companies).

But almost from the moment we finalized our contingency plan, signs began to accumulate that this war would be very different. The politics of the U.S.-created anti-Iraq coalition made it imperative that Israel stay out of the war. Yet for that very reason it was in Saddam Hussein's interest to provoke Israel to intervene. By September, U.S. satellites had detected the transport of ballistic missiles to western Iraq—a mere seven minutes' flight time from Tel Aviv. Israeli defense officials were saying that chemical attacks on the country's major population centers were likely, a belief that was confirmed when the government leased two batteries of Patriot anti-aircraft missiles (adapted for use against ballistic missiles) from the United States. Instead of being behind the lines of the war zone (something we were used to), we ran the risk of *being* the war zone.

In October, tensions mounted when the government issued every Israeli a personal protection kit, complete with gas mask and atropine injectors to combat chemical poisoning. Families were also instructed to create sealed rooms in their houses and apartments with plastic sheeting and masking tape. There was something about receiving those kits, being instructed to carry your gas mask with you wherever you went, having to prepare a sealed room, that brought the uncertainty and potential danger of the situation home in a palpable way.

By the turn of the year, as the U.S.-set January 15 deadline for Iraqi withdrawal from Kuwait drew near, my disquiet had grown. Many airlines suspended flights to Israel. The governments of the

United States and Great Britain advised their nationals to consider leaving the country. Then on the fifteenth itself the Israeli government announced that all schools would be closed for the rest of the week. Slowly it was dawning on me that our contingency plan might be irrelevant to what was likely to be anything but an ordinary war.

Yet despite all these warning signs, it still came as a complete surprise when I woke up on Wednesday, January 16, to the news on the radio that in anticipation of the start of hostilities and likely missile attacks, the Israeli Civil Defense authority was instructing businesses to close and everyone but essential emergency personnel to remain home. It was only then that I fully understood: we were facing a completely different kind of problem than the one we had anticipated. This wasn't just a matter of a call-up of reserves. The government was telling us that *nobody* should come to work. I immediately called a meeting of the task force at the Jerusalem fab.

A Question of Survival

In the twenty minutes it took me to drive from my home in the historic village of Ein Karem on the southwestern outskirts of Jerusalem to the plant in the Har Hotzvim Industrial District, I kept revisiting in my mind the logic of what I was about to do. It seemed almost irresponsible to be worrying about business in the midst of potential physical danger. Yet if I didn't think about the possible consequences, who would?

I was convinced that a complete shutdown of our operations threatened the long-term survival of Intel Israel. Managing a major unit in a global corporation is a continuous fight for resources. When we first proposed setting up the Jerusalem fab in the early 1980s, we were put in competition with Ireland to see which country could develop the better proposal. We had won that round, and by the early '90s we were already starting the process of

negotiating and lobbying inside Intel to convince senior management to expand the Jerusalem fab.

I knew Intel's leaders well and had good relations with them.
I had worked with Andy Grove at Fairchild and had been among
the first generation of employees after Gordon Moore and Bob
Noyce founded Intel in 1968. I was confident that if we had to
interrupt production due to the war, executives in Santa Clara
would understand. I wasn't worried that there would be a negative
impact in the short term.

But as Intel grew larger, decision making was becoming more
decentralized. The key stumbling block to further investment in
Israel was the lingering impression of geopolitical instability in the
region. Indeed, we had already had a number of struggles inside
the company over the transfer of strategic technologies and critical products to the Israeli operation. Therefore I was convinced
that if we had to interrupt production, even for a brief period of
time, we would pay a serious price over the long term.

I had had a glimpse of the risks during a phone conversation
with Intel's then executive vice president, Craig Barrett, the previous September. Barrett was on a stopover in Amsterdam on his
way to Israel for a routine annual operations review. But he called
to tell me that he was considering canceling the trip. "Grove [then
Intel's CEO] is worried about my coming to Israel," he told me.
"He thinks it's too dangerous." Although I convinced him that it
was safe, and he continued his trip as planned, the call provoked a
twinge in my gut. If Intel's senior executives were seeing Israel as
unsafe, what would that mean for our business?

My concern wasn't only for the survival of Intel Israel. It was
also for the survival of Israel's emerging high-tech sector. Intel
Israel was a key anchor of Israel's still small high-tech economy.
If we couldn't operate in an emergency situation, the trust of
multinationals and venture capitalists in the stability of the Israeli
business environment might crumble.

So as I drove to the task-force meeting, I made a quick decision.
We weren't going to take the easy way out. We would ignore the

civil defense instruction. We were going to ask our people to come to work.

Thinking Differently

"This is a completely different situation," I said at the start of the task-force meeting on Wednesday afternoon, "so let's think differently." The first thing we did was to throw out our contingency plan. The next was to ask how we could keep operations going despite the civil defense directive.

In Israel, there is an official category of businesses known as MELACH (an acronym for *Meshek Lishe'at Cherum'* or "economic infrastructure in a state of emergency"). These companies—for example, utilities, defense contractors, the national telecommunications network, and the like—are designated as essential for the ongoing functioning of the economy and are allowed to operate even during officially declared national emergencies. But we didn't have that legal status. The fact is, we had thought about applying for it in the past but just never gotten around to it. It had been pushed aside by more immediate and, at the time, more pressing concerns. And even if we applied for this essential-industry status right away, under the current circumstances who knew how long it would take to receive it? We decided we were going to act like we already had it until and unless somebody told us otherwise.

For three hours, we discussed the full range of risks that remaining opened entailed. The main risk, obviously, was the potential injury of any of our employees on their way to and from work. People had sealed rooms at home, and we had created them in all our main facilities, including the Jerusalem fab. But what about during their daily commute? This was complicated by the fact that we had a contract with a private transportation company to bring our employees to work at the Jerusalem fab, so if we were going to remain open, not only our own employees but also the transport company's employees would be at risk. I weighed the physical risk to our employees and contractors heavily, but in the end concluded that if it was safe enough for employees at the utility company and the phone company to travel to work, there was absolutely no reason why we shouldn't risk it as well.

At the Wednesday task-force meeting there were few objections to the idea of remaining open. To be honest, the whole prospect of missile attacks seemed so theoretical as to be literally impossible to imagine, almost unreal. In the end we decided that we would issue a "call" for Intel employees to continue to come to work—a recommendation, not an order. No one would be punished if they decided to stay home. I made it extremely clear to my direct reports that there would be no coercion. No manager was to pressure employees to come to work who did not want to do so.

This prohibition was especially important to me—and not just for ethical reasons. The problem with coercion is that it often leads to backlash, creating the very resistance that it is meant to overcome. When you order people to do something, their first reaction is often "Wait a minute, if they have to force me, there must be a problem with the whole thing." I knew that I couldn't control every single action of all my managers. But I could make it clear that there would be no direct pressure. At the same time, I was confident that we had embedded a strong instinct for survival in our organizational culture and that people would respond. "Let the Intel Israel culture do its work," I advised. After all, peer pressure is the most powerful motivator.

We would also make it clear that keeping Intel Israel open for business was critical to the future success not only of the organization but also of Israel's high-tech economy. I believed strongly that the only way I could expect Israelis to take a risk was if doing so was critical to the country, not just to the company.

We communicated our decision to the workforce on Wednesday. On the following day, with still no sign of missile attacks, turnout was relatively normal. But that Thursday, January 17, was also the start of the allied bombardment of Iraq. What only one day earlier had seemed like a theoretical possibility would very quickly become reality.

The First Attack

At 2:00 in the morning on Friday, January 18, I was awakened by the sound of an air-raid siren. I joined my wife and teenage children in the sealed room of our Jerusalem home and listened to the radio for the news. Eight missiles had landed in Tel Aviv and Haifa; as far as the authorities could tell, there were no chemical warheads. I got on the phone to the members of the task force and told them to meet me at the plant. I grabbed my gas mask and headed out into the night for the Jerusalem fab.

When I arrived around 3:30, work in the cleanroom had already resumed. At the sound of the alarm, the employees had evacuated to the sealed room, except for a few who agreed to stay behind to operate some etching machines that needed continuous human presence to keep the flow of materials going. After the report that the missiles had landed, employees were given the opportunity to call home before returning to the cleanroom. Things were tense, but relatively normal.

When the task force convened, we reaffirmed the decision to call people to work. Managers had to be contacted and instructed what to say to their staff. Employees had to be called and told that the plant would indeed be open. The transportation company needed to devise alternate routes to get around police roadblocks. In the chaos of a crisis situation, clear communications are especially important. So we spent the bulk of our time planning exactly what to say to our workforce and coordinating our communications with our counterparts in Intel in the United States, who would be wondering what impact the missile attack was having on our operations.

Some 75 percent of the employees on the 7:00 AM shift made it to the plant. Although I hadn't told anyone, I had been expecting maybe 50 percent. The relatively high turnout was a major endorsement of our decision.

That night, after being at the plant for nearly sixteen hours straight, I called Intel senior executives in Santa Clara. I stayed at the plant because I didn't want to call them from my home. I had no idea what their reaction was going to be, and I wanted them to see that Intel Israel was operating as normal—or as close to normal—as possible under the circumstances. I explained that we had decided to remain open, but we weren't forcing any employees to come to work who didn't feel comfortable doing so, and that so far turnout was quite good. They asked a lot of questions; we discussed the potential risks. But in the end they were 7,500 miles away. Under the circumstances, they simply had to trust us.

"Scud Business as Usual"

The second Scud attack came the following night, early on Saturday. No one was killed, but some people were injured. And Intel's employees kept coming to work. When the design center in Haifa opened on Sunday (the first day of the normal Israeli work-week), turnout was up to 80 percent.

After the first few days, we entered a period that I took to calling "Scud business as usual." Attacks continued to happen. On Tuesday night, for example, after two days with no Scuds, there was an especially destructive attack outside of Tel Aviv that led to the deaths of four people, wounded ninety-six, and left hundreds homeless. But we carried on as if everything were normal, and no one tried to stop us. By the middle of the week, the civil defense authority was urging all Israelis to go back to work, so the fact that we were open for business was no longer so unusual. Still, because the schools remained closed, absenteeism at most businesses remained extremely high. The stress was enormous, and I and my team did all we could to boost employee morale.

As our actions on the night of the first attack suggest, constant communication was essential. The task force met daily to assess the rapidly changing situation and plan our communications for the day. We used every means we could—phone, email, on-site meetings, face-to-face conversations—to keep our employees informed of the latest developments. I was traveling continuously among the three Intel sites in Israel—the fab in Jerusalem, the design center in Haifa, and our small sales-and-marketing operation in Tel Aviv—to meet with managers and employees in cafeterias and on production lines. I felt it was essential that I, as the organization's leader, be present to employees "in the flesh." Over and over again, I tried to make three points: first, to reinforce employees' sense of pride at what they were accomplishing; second, to remind them that we weren't out of the woods yet—as far as we knew, the worst might still be yet to come; and third, to stress that this largely unforeseen crisis was also an enormous opportunity and we had to take advantage of it. It was time to show Intel and Israel what we could do.

We also took great care in our communications to global Intel to keep senior executives informed of the developments on the ground in Israel. After the first few days of attacks, I sent a comprehensive email to Intel senior management describing how we were meeting the "war challenge" and delivering on our commitments to the corporation. Andy Grove sent us an extremely supportive letter in response, which I had posted on bulletin boards throughout the organization. His strong public endorsement had an enormous positive impact on employee morale.

Today, some fifteen years later, the decision to continue with business as usual may not seem so radical. At the time, however, it was pretty controversial. In the white heat of the first few days of crisis, everybody operated on instinct. People were so busy that they barely had time to think. But once things settled down into "Scud business as usual," some doubts and questioning began to emerge.

Some saw the decision to remain open as an act of courageous leadership, but others viewed it as an unnecessary risk, literally playing with the lives of employees. Some wondered how we could justify risking people's lives for a company that wasn't even Israeli. Relatively few people actually refused to come to work, but some were bitter for quite a while. And one individual, who did refuse to come to work—and not only during the first week, but also in subsequent weeks after the civil defense directive had been withdrawn—eventually had to be let go.

But these complaints never really cohered into full-fledged opposition to the decision. For one thing, whatever doubts some people had, there was the basic fact that the vast majority of employees had indeed shown up. A successful risk is seldom challenged in retrospect.

In the years since the war, I have often wondered why so many answered the call. Partly, I suspect, it was because coming to work was a welcome alternative to the psychological paralysis brought about by first the prospect and then the reality of the missile strikes. One of the advantages of doing the unexpected is that it can have a galvanizing effect. It shakes people out of their passivity and helps mobilize them for action. At Intel Israel, our bias to go against the current made it natural to decide to remain open even though most businesses in Israel suspended operations. It was the perfect antidote to terror.

Another part of it, I think, is that the call didn't come in a vacuum. We had been talking for years about the imperative of survival and the need to do whatever it takes to be the best. So though not everyone may have agreed with the decision to keep operations open, most understood why we were doing it and trusted that we had the best interests of the people and the organization at heart.

Another important lesson I learned during this period was that when it comes to leading in a crisis, good instincts are a lot more important than good planning. The problem with chaotic situations like war is not so much that you can't anticipate everything—it's that you really can't anticipate *anything*. All you can do is trust your instincts, embrace the chaos, and then deal with the consequences as they emerge.

One issue, for instance, that I completely underestimated was the impact of my decision on our employees' families. To her credit, my head of human resources had raised the issue early on. The only woman on the crisis task force, and a mother, she was sensitive to the implications of our decision for our female workforce (about half of the employees at the Jerusalem fab were women). I remember her asking, at the task-force meeting when we decided to remain open, "Can we really ask mothers to be separated from their children during the threat of missile attacks?"

At the time I didn't exactly dismiss her question. But in the total scheme of things, dealing with the family fallout was not my highest priority. I felt that such separations were inevitable in a situation in which the "front" was potentially everywhere.

Her concerns, however, turned out to be prescient. A few days into the attacks, a manager at the Jerusalem fab reported that the lobby was crawling with young children. Some of our employees, especially women, were bringing their kids to work. After all, the schools were still closed and, just as my HR head had predicted, people didn't want to be separated from their children in case of an attack.

But here is the great thing about embracing the chaos. Faced with this unanticipated development, the organization responded, almost automatically, by temporarily entering the child-care business. Local managers in Jerusalem set up a day-care center in a support building of the fab. It had never occurred to anybody on the task force (including my HR head) that establishing a temporary day-care center for employees' children might be a good thing to do. But once faced with the fact that concerned parents were bringing their children to work, it was an obvious step to take. Throughout the Scud attacks, on any given day as many as fifty children were in the center.

Throughout the war, there were a lot of examples at Intel Israel of this kind of improvisational everyday heroism. For me, one story best captures the way the organization rose to the occasion. A team from the Haifa design center was on a conference call with its U.S. counterparts when the alarm signaling a Scud attack began to sound. To the amazement of their U.S. colleagues, they calmly asked for a brief interruption in the meeting so they could move to the site's sealed room, located in the computer center, then resumed the call a few minutes later as if nothing had happened.

Delivering—No Matter What

The last Scud attack took place on February 25, not quite six weeks after the bombardment of Iraq had begun and one day after the start of the ground war. On Thursday, February 28, the Israeli state of emergency officially ended. All told, some thirty-nine Scuds in eighteen separate attacks landed on Israeli territory during the five and a half weeks, none carrying chemical warheads. Although only one person was killed directly by an attack, seventy-four people died of indirect causes—for example, from heart attacks brought on by the missile strikes or by suffocation due to improper use of protective gear. More than two hundred were wounded by blasts, flying glass, and shrapnel. Property damage to some 4,000 buildings was in the millions of dollars. And some 1,600 families had to be evacuated.[1]

The war had indirect economic costs as well. According to the Israeli Ministry of Finance, industrial output during the war was at about 75 percent of its normal level. The costs to the Israeli economy in lost output totaled approximately $3 billion.

At Intel Israel, we were extremely fortunate. None of the Scuds landed in the Jerusalem area where most of our people worked. No Intel employee or family member was injured or rendered homeless by the attacks. And in terms of the economic impact, both the Jerusalem fab and the Haifa design center were able to meet all of their manufacturing and product development commitments.

The thing about chaos is that there is no good information. We had spent a lot of time and energy during the crisis trying to anticipate the legal ramifications of disobeying the government's instruction to close down. Imagine my surprise when I learned, weeks after the attacks began, that the civil defense directive to stay home from work had the status of only a recommendation, not a legally binding order. At the time, most people, ourselves included, had assumed exactly the opposite. So our decision to keep operations open was, from a legal point of view, not so risky after all.

To this day, I'm convinced that meeting our commitments to Intel during the First Gulf War was critical to the future evolution of Intel Israel—and, indeed, of the entire Israeli high-tech economy. A few years later, in 1995, Intel invested in its second semiconductor plant in Israel, at Qiryat Gat. In 1999, the Haifa design center won the assignment to develop Intel's Centrino mobile computing technology, which was launched in 2003. And in subsequent years, whenever we got any push-back about doing major projects in Israel, it was always helpful to remind our colleagues that, as the experience during the war had demonstrated, "Intel Israel delivers, no matter what."

What's more, the culture of survival that we created during the First Gulf War has shaped Intel Israel down to the present day. After the initial version of this chapter appeared in the *Harvard Business Review* in December 2006,[2] I received an email from Shuky Erlich, a former Intel Israel colleague and general manager of the Haifa design center during the conflict between Israel and Hezbollah in the summer of 2006. (By the way, Erlich is that software engineer who quit Intel in protest over my no-transfer policy, only to return a few years later.) The war with Hezbollah was especially costly in terms of loss of life and economic disruption to the area along the Lebanese border, including Haifa. And the challenge Erlich faced to keep the business going in the midst of that disruption was similar to the challenge we faced during the First Gulf War. "I found myself looking back more than once to the 1991 crisis and trying to find answers based on what was done in those days," Erlich wrote me. "Even just to set the path for future generations, it was important and dramatic to make the decisions you made at that time. You were my role model during the [recent] crisis."

On the one hand, I was gratified to hear that the leadership lessons we learned during the First Gulf War had taken root in the

Intel Israel culture—so much so that they were still operative after I had retired. On the other, I was sad that due to longstanding failures of political leadership on both sides of the Israeli-Arab conflict, my colleagues still had to confront the challenges of doing business in the middle of a war.

The situation I faced during the First Gulf War was extreme. I sincerely hope that you will never have to face the equivalent in your career. That said, the principles of leadership that the story illustrates are relevant even in more ordinary and less dramatic situations of turbulence. The job of the leader is to insist on survival, act against the current, and leverage random opportunities. In the concluding chapters of this book, I'll discuss some of the supports you need to put in place in order to do so.

5

THE SOFT SKILLS OF
HARD LEADERSHIP

As the story of the First Gulf War suggests, leadership the hard way can be a demanding way of life. It asks a lot of the leader, and it asks a lot of the organization. To meet those demands you need to develop a support infrastructure that will allow you to rise to the occasion. In this chapter, I want to focus on a key part of that infrastructure: what I call the soft skills of hard leadership.

I was trained as an electrical engineer, and for more than thirty years I worked at a no-nonsense high-tech company founded by scientists and engineers. Intel's culture values hard data and objective analysis. It believes in constructive confrontation and "may the best idea win." This is the hard side of business leadership. It's absolutely necessary for success in today's environment.

Yet one of the most important things I learned during my career is that leadership the hard way also requires some extremely soft skills. These skills are so counterintuitive that they can appear to be irrational. As a result, they are easy to devalue and dismiss. Most discussions of leadership ignore them. But in my experience they are just as important as the more readily accepted hard skills of, say, strategic management, process discipline, or quantitative analysis.

Some of these soft skills have to do with what I call the inner life of the leader. The fact is, to lead in the ways that I have been describing so far—insisting on survival, acting against the current, leveraging random opportunities—you need to develop a particular frame of mind, a distinctive way of perceiving and acting. You must free yourself from habitual ways of looking at things, cultivate an independent and questioning perspective, and be ready to embrace alternative and counterintuitive points of view.

Other soft skills concern how leaders interact with their people. To lead the hard way, you need to develop a close bond with your people. In particular, you must know how to use your own behavior as a mode of strategic communication to guide the organization in the direction you want it to go.

Like leadership itself, these soft skills cannot be taught. But once you are aware of their importance, you can begin to learn how to develop and use them.

Freeing Up Time

Now that I am retired, I finally have the opportunity to read. Recently I came upon the following passage by the Roman philosopher Marcus Aurelius. "The greatest part of what we say and do is unnecessary," the philosopher writes in his *Meditations*. As a result, "on every occasion a man should ask himself, is this one of the unnecessary things?"[1]

That's good advice for leaders. Unless you can shed all the unproductive activities that tend to fill up a manager's schedule, you will never have the mental shelf space to develop a fresh perspective on the organization and its challenges. For that reason, the first soft skill is the ability to free up time.

In my opinion, too much unproductive busyness is the bane of the modern manager. Most managers spend a great deal of time thinking about what they plan to do but relatively little time thinking about what they plan *not* to do. As a result, they become so busy, so consumed by the daily round of meetings and reviews, so caught up in fighting the fires of the moment that they cannot really attend to the long-term threats and risks facing the organization. So the first soft skill of leadership the hard way is to cultivate the perspective of Marcus Aurelius: avoid busyness, free up your time, stay focused on what really matters.

Let me put it bluntly: every leader should routinely keep a substantial portion of his or her time—I would say as much as 50 percent—unscheduled. Until you do so, you will never be able to develop the detachment required to identify long-term threats to the organization or the flexibility to move quickly to take advantage of random opportunities as they emerge. Only when you have substantial "slop" in your schedule—unscheduled time—will you have the space to be able to reflect on what you are doing, learn from experience, and recover from your inevitable mistakes.

Leaders without such free time end up tackling issues only when there is an immediate or visible problem. When they free up considerable portions of their time, by contrast, leaders have the capacity to identify and begin to address problems before they blossom into a full-blown crisis.

Managers' typical response to my argument about free time is, "That's all well and good, but here are all the things I have to do." Yet we waste so much time in unproductive activity. It takes enormous effort on the part of the leader to keep time free for the truly important things.

When I was running Intel Israel, I did a variety of things to force managers to free up their time. One of the more controversial was to get rid of their administrative assistants. This may sound paradoxical. After all, isn't the whole point of assistants to help executives manage their time, to make sure that they do not get overwhelmed by the press of daily demands?

That's what I used to think myself. But by the mid-1990s, I was becoming aware that assistants, the very people whose role was to facilitate productive interaction, had actually become an obstacle to it. It wasn't their fault, of course; it was the managers' fault. They saw their assistants as gatekeepers to control the demands on their time. So they gave over control of their schedule to their assistants. But the paradoxical result was that my people were so overscheduled, so busy, that one could barely get any time for meaningful interaction with them! At a certain point, it suddenly dawned on me that the best time to reach my people was in the evening, because they were all booked solid during the day.

At about the same time, laptop computers were just beginning to become a common tool in business organizations. I had been the first executive at Intel to distribute them widely throughout the organization. Every employee at Intel Israel had one. What with email, calendaring programs, and the like, I began to think that we could do without assistants completely. I felt that if I forced my managers to take responsibility for the decisions about how they used their time, they would make better use of it.

When I made the announcement that I was getting rid of administrative assistants, my managers were furious. We had many loud, contentious meetings in which people roundly criticized my decision. Those meetings were tough; I think the only thing that made them bearable was that people didn't really believe I was going to go through with it.

Eventually I came to realize that the only way my managers would give up their assistants was if I gave up mine. I needed to model the kind of behavior that I was asking of my people. So I announced that my assistant of many years was transferring to another job.

Giving up my assistant was the catalyst for a fascinating change in my behavior. I became more direct, more focused on what really mattered. I began interacting with people immediately—in the moment—rather than scheduling formal times to meet with them. When people would come up to me in the cafeteria and say, "I need an hour of your time," I would respond, "I have five minutes right now. What's on your mind?" I estimate that my own availability and efficient use of time increased by at least 50 percent.

Not that being without an assistant didn't cause problems. Of course it did, but that was precisely the point. Confronting those problems forced me to innovate. The result was a transformation in the way I interacted with my people. For example, not long after I got rid of my assistant, I encountered a problem that I had never had to deal with before. I was about to leave on one of my frequent long trips to Intel sites in the United States, and for the first time I faced the prospect of having to manage my voicemail by myself. These trips usually lasted anywhere from ten days to two weeks, and during the period I was gone I would typically receive hundreds of voicemail messages. My assistant had been an enormous help in categorizing these voicemails for me and figuring out which were really important and needed to be answered right away. How to avoid being overwhelmed by the sheer quantity of messages?

The solution I finally came up with was elegantly simple. I changed my voicemail message to say that I would be out of the country for a couple of weeks and to please "leave only urgent messages." Suddenly my voicemail traffic plummeted from hundreds of messages to a handful—and with no discernible degradation in the performance of the Intel Israel organization!

The moral of this story is how easy it is for the time of the leader to be consumed by busy work and that once the busy work is eliminated there is the space for more productive interactions, more long-term thinking, and real work. Some of my managers were never convinced that jettisoning their assistants was a good idea. Yet over time many came to see the value of the change. Interactions among the management team became more direct. Much less time was wasted on non–value-adding activities. Slowly, people began to realize that both their efficiency and their availability went way up.

What happened to the assistants? Freeing up my managers' time resulted in freeing them up for more productive work as well. Many of the assistants had considerable education; some even had advanced degrees. In the vast majority of cases, we were able to place them in more responsible positions in functional areas such as logistics or purchasing.

Of course, an even bigger challenge than freeing up time is figuring out what to do with it once you have it. Most managers are not used to not being busy. In the rest of this chapter, I'll discuss the kind of activities that managers should be focusing on. But the starting point for all these activities is freeing up your time. Remember Marcus Aurelius and always ask: "Is this one of the necessary things?"

The Discipline of Daydreaming

I'm not sure why, but daydreaming has always been a big part of my personality. I suspect it has something to do with the fact that as a child I spent so much time on my own. Whatever the reason, it is a powerful personal inclination. Some people fall asleep during meetings. I daydream. And I have found the habit to be a compelling resource in my role as a leader. That's why I call the second soft skill of leadership the hard way "the discipline of daydreaming."

Nearly every major decision of my business career was, to some degree, the result of daydreaming. The first inklings of the vision to "bring something back to Israel" emerged while daydreaming in my professor's switching-theory class. The concept of the EPROM occurred to me while musing on the anomaly of the floating gate. The decision to locate our first fab in Jerusalem, not in Haifa or Tel Aviv, was the product of blue-sky, "what if?" thinking very close to daydreaming. And the origin of our subsequent decision to locate Intel Israel's second fab in Qiryat Gat was the product of a similar vague impulse to help "develop the South" of Israel. To be sure, in every one of these cases I had to collect a lot of data, do detailed analysis, and make a data-based argument to convince superiors, colleagues, and business partners. But all that came later. In the beginning, there was the daydream.

By daydreaming, I mean loose, unstructured thinking with no particular goal in mind. Daydreaming requires letting your mind go, releasing all constraints—including the constraint of logic! By definition, it's not a linear process. But it can be highly purposeful—an intensive (although unconscious) targeting and then distilling of an idea.

In fact, I believe that daydreaming is a distinctive mode of cognition especially well suited to the complex, "fuzzy" problems that characterize a more turbulent business environment. Daydreaming is a way of knowing, one that is essential for the kind of reframing necessary to perceive and take advantage of random opportunities—as I did when I redefined the floating gate problem as the potential solution for a whole new type of semiconductor memory. It is only when you release your thinking from the constraints of present-day reality that you can come up with truly radical solutions to seemingly intractable problems. In this respect, daydreaming is intimately linked with innovation and improvisation of any kind.

Daydreaming is also an effective means of coping with complexity. When a problem has high degrees of complexity, the level of detail can be overwhelming. The more one focuses on the details, the more one risks becoming lost in them. There are a lot of very smart people in business today who are so detail-oriented that not only can't they see the forest for the trees, they can't even see the trees for the leaves! It's impossible to solve a complex problem only analytically. To see the big picture, sometimes you just have to let your mind go free.

Every child knows how to daydream. But many, perhaps most, lose the capacity as they grow up. Most institutions of society tend to devalue daydreaming. The schools punish students who do it. And in contemporary managerial culture (at least in the West), daydreaming is too often equated with laziness and seen as an unproductive waste of time. Given all of society's taboos against daydreaming, it took me a long time to get comfortable with the idea that daydreaming is a critical discipline of leadership.

You can't really teach someone to daydream, any more than you can teach someone to be a leader. Nor can you schedule it or otherwise plan for it. All you can do is try to be aware of it when it happens—and, when it does, to appreciate it and cultivate it. At Intel Israel, for example, one of the reasons that I sought out people with unusual and, specifically, nontechnical backgrounds was because I felt that diversity would encourage daydreaming.

It's also useful for a leader to make room for experiences designed to jump-start personal reflection and learning. These don't necessarily have to be work-related in any simple or obvious sense. In today's turbulent economy, you never know what kind of input is going to trigger a key insight or idea. Take time to prime the pump for daydreaming.

In my own experience, a variety of activities have been effective catalysts for daydreaming. Some were traditional, like taking time to go to lectures and conferences. For example, it was a lecture by the MIT economist Lester Thurow on global competitiveness that sparked the idea to get rid of administrative assistants at Intel Israel. To be honest, I don't remember exactly what it was that Thurow said that gave me the idea. But his general description of the kind of organization that tended to be successful in the new, more competitive global economy definitely got me thinking of ways to make our organization leaner and more effective.

Another way I stimulated my thinking was to make an effort to stay in touch with environments and subcultures that were outside the usual circles I traveled in as a business executive. For instance, at one point I agreed that Intel Israel would sponsor a classical music series in the Red Sea town of Eilat. And for a time I served on the board of an Israeli non-profit foundation that used government money to fund documentary film projects throughout the country. I made these commitments only partly because I was interested in music and documentary film-making. They were also a way for me to interact with types of people that I would never meet on the job—artists, musicians, film-makers, and the like. These interactions helped stimulate my own creativity and my capacity to see my own situation in fresh ways.

Finally, I always tried to make time for a few personal avocations that would take me completely away from my day-to-day life at Intel and put me into a totally different space. I think that is partly why I took up flying at midlife. I have also been an avid motorcyclist. And to this day I am an active bicyclist. I find that alone in the cockpit at ten thousand feet or out on the road cycling through the Judean hills or in the Italian Dolomites is one of my best times for letting my mind go free. I often come back with unexpected new ideas or crazy notions that I want to explore more systematically.

So my advice is this: try to be aware when you are daydreaming, and instead of fighting it, nurture it. And try not to discourage or suppress it in your organization. The next time you ask a question at a meeting and nobody answers, don't automatically assume that no one is paying attention. Maybe they're daydreaming. Who knows, some good may come from it!

Trusting—and Testing—Intuitions

Daydreaming gives birth to intuitions, ideas, or conclusions that arise with seemingly little effort and with little or no conscious deliberation. A third soft skill that leaders need to learn is how to trust their intuitions and use them more actively as the basis for decisions. When you are flying through a thunderstorm, you have to act quickly, in the moment, and without necessarily analyzing what you are doing.

A great deal of recent cognitive science research on how the mind processes information has shown that much of our everyday thinking, feeling, and acting operates outside our conscious awareness.[2] Our explicit analytical knowledge is just the tip of the iceberg. Below the surface there is a vast realm of tacit knowledge that we develop without even being aware of it. Especially in innovation-based businesses, this tacit knowledge—the kind that can't be easily codified (nor, therefore, easily copied by competitors)—turns out to be far more important than most organizations think.[3]

Yet in most business organizations, intuitive thinking still has a bad rap. At Intel, for example, people tended to mistrust intuitive decision making—what they termed, disparagingly, "seat-of-the-pants" management. The common attitude was "Show me the data." I would never argue for a manager to ignore data. But leaders increasingly face situations in which they don't have all the data, or the data are ambiguous, or the change they are contemplating is so radical that it's not yet clear what would even qualify as data. In such situations, it's important to let intuition be your guide. As Albert Einstein once said, "Not everything that can be counted counts, and not everything that counts can be counted."[4]

Of course, not all intuitions are necessarily good ones. Just as intuition can easily be a source of new insight, it can also lead us astray. So in addition to trusting your intuitions, you must also test them rigorously. Indeed, I would say that systematically test- ing intuitions is a big part of the process of trusting them. If you don't value your intuitions enough to bring them into the cold light of day and confront them with reality, then maybe they are not so sound after all. To effectively harness intuition, you need a double loop. You need to test your intuitions and continuously revise them in the light of what you learn.

Take, for example, the story that I told in Chapter Two about switching the heads of the Haifa design center and the Jerusalem fab. I had an intuition about the potential value of developing more well-rounded, multidisciplinary managers through a program of lateral transfers. I was right to trust that basic intuition. Yet I didn't really test it in advance. For example, I made the job change without consulting any of the Intel managers back in the States who were responsible for running the company's design and manufacturing functions worldwide. I was worried that if I started consulting people, that would be an open invitation for them to come up with reasons not to make the change.

It took the failure of the manager assigned to run the Haifa center for me to realize the important elements that I had left out of my plan—specifically, the need for extensive senior-management support to help the transferred managers learn the culture of the new units they were running. To be sure, I learned from this mistake and changed the transfer program accordingly, but that knowledge came at a very high cost: the failure (and, ulti- mately, the loss to the company) of a good manager. In retrospect, it would have been far better to find ways to test my intuition before plunging ahead with the transfer program.

One way to make sure you test your intuition is to create and encourage a culture of dissent. By promoting strong people who will stand up to you and say no, you can create an environment in which your intuitions have to run the gauntlet of constructive criticism. For example, there was one veteran employee at the Haifa design center who was challenging me all the time. To be honest, I had extremely ambivalent feelings about this individual. It's no fun to be constantly challenged and criticized. Yet in the end I was glad he was there. He kept me on my toes.

Encouraging and welcoming challenges to your intuitions doesn't necessarily mean always backing down. It's a balancing act—remaining true to your core intuitions even as you take into account disagreement and adapt your ideas to criticism and dissent. Indeed, the stronger you are as a leader, the less likely it is that you will back down and the harder it will be for your people to challenge you—which is all the more reason to surround yourself with strong people who will push their own points of view just as persistently as you do your own.

By definition, intuitive knowledge cannot be taught. Rather, it is the product of an individual's specific experiences. But it is possible to educate your intuitions—for example, by actively seeking out feedback, by exposing yourself to new situations and new environments that will spark your learning, by systematically exploring the connections between seemingly unrelated phenomena, or by carefully considering the trade-offs between alternative courses of action.[5] But the first step is to trust your intuitions and use them to inform your actions.

Communicating Through Behavior

So far, the soft skills I have discussed concern the internal mindset of the leader. But leadership the hard way isn't just personal; it is also interpersonal. It requires close bonds with your people. Take the example of my experience during the First Gulf War. There was no way the people of Intel Israel would have responded to my call and kept working if they didn't already trust that I had their best interests at heart.

How does the leader build that trust? One important way is by staying true to shared values. Indeed, values are so important that

I will discuss them in a separate chapter. Another way is through continuous communication—like the high-bandwidth communication we engaged in during the First Gulf War. But what I want to focus on here is something different: the way leaders must use their behavior strategically in their interactions with their people.

Leadership is about action. A leader needs to act in order to get things done. But action is also a form of communication. There are many situations in which a leader acts in a certain way to communicate his vision and values for the organization. The final soft skill you as a leader must cultivate is becoming aware of the impact of your behavior on the organization—and using that behavior, strategically, to move the organization in the direction in which you want it to go.

One of the most difficult things for most leaders to understand is just how sensitive the organization is to every move that the leader makes, every perturbation of style or mood. The eyes of the organization are always on you. People will watch your every step and emulate what you do. This is a powerful tool in the sense that the leader's behavior helps create the organization's culture. Everything you do will be reflected in the organization. But unless you cultivate a double awareness about your behavior, you can end up doing things that inadvertently contradict what you say and what you intend.

It took me years to realize just how powerful an impact my actions could have on employees at Intel Israel. Once, for example, I chewed out a subordinate at a team meeting for some error (I forget what). At the next meeting of the group, the individual didn't show up. I asked a colleague where the missing manager was—only to be informed that he had been so upset at my criticism that he had become ill!

Another time, lost in thought, I passed a colleague in the hallway without saying hello. It was only later that I learned that my silence had caused him considerable anxiety. Had he done something wrong? Was he no longer on my good side? My non-response, which was completely inadvertent, made him genuinely worried that he had done something to damage his standing in the organization.

Or consider my decision to eliminate administrative assistants. When I first announced the change, I couldn't understand why nothing was happening. As strange as it may sound in retrospect, it took me three months to figure out that until I removed my *own* assistant, nobody else was going to make the change. They just didn't take it seriously. It was only by acting that I could make real the seriousness of my intention.

As I became more aware of the impact of my behavior, I tried to use it consciously not just to get things done but also explicitly to send a message. In 1982, for example, during the construction of the Jerusalem fab, I arranged for a three-month stay at an Intel fab in Beaverton, Oregon, to learn the ins and outs of semiconductor manufacturing management. Because the stay would be relatively long, my wife and children were coming with me, and we had rented an apartment in Beaverton. A few days before we left, however, I heard news from Intel corporate that complicated my plans.

The early '80s were a difficult period for Intel. The semiconductor industry was mired in recession, and the downturn had had a strong negative impact on Intel's financial health. In 1981, for example, sales and profits had declined precipitously, for the first time in the company's history, and Intel's market cap was cut nearly in half. And in 1982 Intel's key customer, IBM, bought 20 percent of the company on the theory that a major cash infusion was necessary to ensure its survival. As part of the internal effort to deal with hard times, Intel instituted an across-the-board 10 percent pay cut. The announcement of the new plan was scheduled for a few days after my departure.

The timing posed a personal dilemma. I felt it was essential that I, as Intel Israel's leader, deliver the bad news myself—not fob the task off on my subordinates. Yet if I delayed my departure, especially without explaining why, people would know that something was up. I suppose I could have organized a conference call and announced the news to the Intel Israel staff from Oregon, but frankly I didn't even consider it. At this moment of uncertainty and crisis, I strongly believed I needed to be present "in the flesh." So, much as I hated to admit it to myself, what I had to do was clear: I flew to Oregon with my family, as scheduled, got them settled in our apartment there, and then immediately flew back to Israel to personally make the announcement of the pay cut. After informing my people and dealing with all the fallout, I got on a plane again and returned to Oregon to take up my assignment there.

Another way in which I would frequently use my behavior strategically was to intervene selectively in decisions and processes down in the organization on issues that I considered of strategic importance. I'm not particularly detail-oriented and am probably the last person anyone would describe as a micromanager. Yet at certain key points in my time as the leader of Intel Israel, I chose to go deeply into aspects of the organization's management to communicate the importance of a particular initiative or plan. One example was the decision, described in Chapter Two, to hire a more diverse workforce. There was a period of time in the mid-1990s when I was regularly reviewing—and sometimes reversing—hiring decisions.

Another area in which I felt it was essential to be actively involved was the negotiations with the Israeli government for both the Jerusalem and Qiryat Gat fabs. Especially in the latter case, where I had a full team to support me, I could easily have left the negotiations to the team until things had reached the ministerial level. Instead, I handled them personally. It wasn't that I didn't trust my team. It's just that, given the importance of the investment to the future of Intel Israel, I felt my presence as the leader was essential in order to communicate to everyone—the organization, the Israeli government, municipal authorities, Intel corporate—just how committed I was to completing the deal successfully.

Sometimes a leader's symbolic actions need to be dramatic—and maybe even a little bit crazy. For instance, I am viscerally opposed to the idea of using compensation as a means to motivate people. I get suspicious of anyone who seems to be in it primarily for the money. I wanted to attract people to Intel Israel who could really get excited about our values and our mission, not just look on us as a place to make more money. In fact, I felt so strongly about this principle that I instituted a policy of never discussing salary with a potential new hire until we were ready to make a definitive offer to bring the person on board. That was normal practice in the high-tech industry for most professional jobs, but it was highly unusual for the hourly jobs in semiconductor fabrication plants.

One time, we made an offer to someone for a senior leadership position at Intel Israel. Before accepting, he said that he wanted to talk directly to me. When we met, the individual explained that in principle he accepted the offer. But he had a lot of questions about "fringe benefits." For example, what about transportation? Could he have a company car? His list went on and on. When he finished, I responded simply: "I appreciate your concerns—so much so that I'm withdrawing the offer. I just don't think you'll fit in here."

Of course, my response wasn't *purely* symbolic. I really did believe that the new hire wouldn't fit in at Intel Israel. Still, I acted the way I did, at least in part, to deliver a message to the organization about the kind of culture we wanted to create and the kind of people we wanted to hire. I was keenly aware that my behavior was a powerful form of organizational communication.

A leader has to be careful with this kind of symbolic action. If you become too conscious about always trying to make an impression, you can risk becoming inauthentic—even manipulative. If the organization believes that your actions are "just an act," they are likely to have the opposite effect of what you intend. But as long as your actions are consistent with your vision and values, then they are likely to be perceived as genuine.

Freeing up time; the discipline of daydreaming; trusting, but also testing, one's intuitions; using one's behavior strategically—all these soft skills will rarely show up in the typical course on leadership. Yet in my experience they are essential for becoming the kind of leader who can succeed in turbulent times. Without them, I wouldn't have been able to lead Intel Israel in the way that I did.

6

MAKING VALUES REAL

In a world characterized by turbulence, every organization needs a solid anchor, some unchanging core that remains the same no matter how disruptive the environment gets. That anchor is the organization's values. Markets and competitors, technology and business models—all may change, some even radically, over time. But once an organization defines its values, those values should not change. They are an important reference point for orienting the organization to the long term. They provide the stability and continuity that allow an organization to adapt to new circumstances.

With the increasing turbulence of the world economy, more and more attention has been paid to the critical role of values in driving competitive success.[1] Yet at the same time that so many business leaders are talking about values, we are also seeing massive breakdowns of ethical behavior at many large corporations. Witness the widespread corporate fraud of a few years ago that brought down companies such as Enron, or the more recent scandals involving the backdating of stock options by CEOs and other senior executives. Apparently, at the precise moment when companies are finding values so essential they are also finding it more difficult to live up to them.

It is really not so paradoxical when you think about it. The same forces that are making values so important are also increasing the pressures to violate them. In an environment in which the rules are always changing and threats to survival are frequent, it's natural for people to start thinking that they must "do anything" to survive. There is an enormous temptation to cut corners, take the easy way out, or look the other way when behavior enters that murky gray area where value violations tend to happen. In the middle of a thunderstorm, it becomes far easier to imperceptibly cross over an ethical line.

The problem is, such shortcuts often bring about precisely the opposite of what leaders intend, trapping companies in a vicious circle. An inclination to "do anything," for example, not only tends to mire an organization in short-term thinking, but sooner or later it also becomes a convenient excuse for more everyday vices such as greed, power, and corruption. As a result, the very actions taken to ensure survival end up making it *less* likely, not more. If more executives at Enron had had genuine integrity, the company might still be around today.

This vicious circle doesn't occur only in the business world. Consider the U.S. government's so-called war on terror. The Bush administration used the American public's fears about survival, stimulated by the attacks on 9/11, to argue that we live in a different and more dangerous world, one that requires taking shortcuts around longstanding traditions and practices: shortcuts such as curtailing civil liberties, creating a special extrajudicial legal regime for detainees, ignoring the Geneva Conventions, even embracing torture. But these shortcuts have ended up violating some of the fundamental values of the U.S. Constitution. Not only have they been ineffective, they have also been used as the cover for rampant political opportunism, corruption, and abuse. As a result, the much vaunted war on terror has ended up degrading many of the very values that it was supposed to protect—and, I fear, caused serious long-term damage to America's standing in the world.

So although I believe that staying true to an organization's values is an essential tool for navigating the turbulence of the current economic environment, I'm also realistic enough (and perhaps pessimistic enough) to realize that value violations are not rare, but common. Therefore leaders must be relentless—and sometimes even obsessive—about making the organization's values real. Not only must they establish the highest ethical standards; they must also create a culture of transparency that surfaces such violations when they occur, so the organization can recover from them.

Being Relentless About Values

At Intel Israel we had a values statement that, like the value statements at most organizations, rounded up all the usual suspects. It was full of high-sounding but generic phrases about "respect for people," "results orientation," "quality," and the like. I believe that words matter if for no other reason than that they highlight the distance between the way things are and the way they are supposed to be. But even the best words can become so corrupted that they get turned inside out and end up encouraging behavior the very opposite of what they intend.

Take, for instance, the idea of an "orientation to results." If a company isn't careful, having an orientation to results can quickly end up meaning "the ends justify the means." As soon as there is any problem with producing results, people are immediately tempted to start sandbagging their plans, falsifying performance data, and the like. When a leader lets such behavior go on, an organization will lose its competitiveness over the long term.

So my approach was always to focus on what it would take to make the words real as reflected in the behavior of our people. I took this task so seriously in part because one of the biggest challenges in creating Intel Israel was implanting Intel's high levels of integrity in a country where the traditional business culture involved a lot of cutting of ethical corners. The Israeli business environment is pretty freewheeling. There is a much greater tendency on the part of companies there than in the United States to engage in activities that skirt the law. In my experience, for example, an Israeli company is far more likely to try to get around the laws governing corporate taxation than a typical American company. The basic attitude is "let's try it; the worst thing that can happen is we get caught—in which case, either we pay the fine or try to fight it in court and see what happens."

I refused to engage in such practices. My attitude was that Intel Israel would follow the very highest standards, no matter what the practices of the local business culture might be. In the early days I had many clashes inside Intel Israel over this issue. People would ask, "Why don't we do things like other companies do?"

Let me give you what may seem like a relatively minor example. It's common practice in Israel for companies to give employees gifts on major holidays such as New Year's or Passover. Typically, the process works like this: a company cuts a deal with a big department store that, in exchange for major discounts on a range of products, has a monopoly over the gift selections at the company. The department store brings the range of qualifying gifts into the workplace and employees select the ones that they want. Although the gift is clearly an employee benefit (and sometimes worth considerable amounts of money), the employee pays no taxes on the gifts, and the company writes off the cost as a business expense.

We participated in this practice for a while, but it always made me uncomfortable. Finally, at a certain point I simply said, "Let's stop this circus and just give people money instead" (which, of course, would have to be declared as income). It was a big shock for people, both inside and outside the company. "Intel doesn't give presents!"

Other ethical dilemmas were not so minor. My uncompromising approach to the organization's values could affect major business decisions on which millions of dollars of investment were riding. When we were defining the Qiryat Gat fab incentive package, for example, the government negotiators asked for something that from their perspective was perfectly innocuous. A key raison d'être of the deal was to encourage economic development in Israel, so the government asked us to commit to certain targets for "local content" (that is, coming from Israel-based companies) in both the construction budget for the plant and the third-party supplier budget once production commenced.

It wasn't an unreasonable request. After all, in arguing for government support for the plant, I had made a big deal myself about the benefits to the Israeli economy. Yet I had a big problem with the proposal. At Intel, one of our values is that when we make a commitment, we keep it. In other words, whatever we commit to, we do. But it wasn't at all clear that committing to local content to the extent the government wanted made economic sense. For example, at that point we didn't yet know whether the Israeli construction industry could handle a complex construction project like that of the Qiryat Gat fab. As for the supplier budget, we didn't even know what product we would be making. It was simply too early to determine how much local content we could use. If it made business sense to use local suppliers, of course we would be inclined to do it. But at that stage of the game I wasn't going to commit to hard-and-fast numbers. So I refused.

As an alternative, I proposed language to the effect that Intel would use its "best efforts" to find, develop, and do business with local suppliers. Moreover, I argued that emphasizing "best efforts" would be more effective than any defined targets in stimulating the organization to work with local suppliers.

The government negotiators weren't buying it. They insisted on clearly defined targets and commitments—so much so that the impasse threatened to undermine the entire negotiation. But I remained steadfast in my refusal because I knew that if I brought such a commitment back to the organization, my people would know that it wasn't realistic—and this would undermine the organization's commitment to delivering on its promises.

In the end the government backed down. The negotiators agreed to the softer language—on the condition that the government could closely monitor our performance over time. As I had initially suspected, we ended up exceeding the proposed targets that the government had demanded within the first five years of the fab's existence. But the key point is this: I was fully prepared to walk away from the deal if the government had insisted on its proposal.

Another issue over which I clashed with the government (and with my own people) concerned temporary employment incentives. At a number of points during the period that I was running

Intel Israel, the Israeli government set up temporary programs to give companies financial incentives to hire people. For every new employee a company took on it would receive a subsidy from the government. These subsidies could add up to substantial sums of money.

I refused to accept them. My people couldn't believe it, but as far as I was concerned, my logic was clear: we didn't hire anybody unless there was a clear business need for hiring them. And if it made economic and business sense to hire someone, then I was willing to pay whatever it took to get them. If Intel Israel accepted the government's employment subsidies, then soon enough we would start hiring people we didn't really need—just to receive the subsidy. But at some point in the future, I knew, the subsidies would disappear, and we would be left with employees that would be an economic burden on the organization and that we would have to let go. That wasn't ethical—either for Intel Israel or for the individuals involved. It certainly did not display respect for people.

People thought I was being rigid. But the thing to understand is that in Israel at the time, the government's policy had led to a lot of shady dealings—and, in some cases, outright cheating—on the part of companies to maximize the subsidy they received. We weren't going to play that game.

It wasn't that I was opposed in principle to the idea of government incentives. After all, we had received incentives to locate our fabs in Jerusalem and Qiryat Gat. I believed strongly (and still do) that such incentives were both a legitimate means for Israel to compete effectively with other countries in the competition for multinational investment and a kind of necessary risk premium to compensate for the geopolitical instability of the region. But when a company starts using temporary incentives to lower the effective wage rate of its operation, that undermines long-term competitiveness.

A funny thing happened with these employment incentives. In one case, it turns out that even though we refused them, the government paid them to us anyway. So we found ourselves with over half a million dollars that we didn't quite know what to do with. "Should we return the money?" my finance people asked me.

In this case, I decided that I had made my point and wasn't going to be a fanatic about it. If the government was going to go out of its way to pay us, despite my refusal to participate in the subsidy program, we weren't going to return the money. But I wasn't going to let it flow to our top line either. Instead, we used the money to set up a special fund to provide our employees with low-interest loans, mainly for housing.

Saying "No"

As these examples suggest, in many situations the key to staying true to your values is not so much doing something as *not* doing something—saying "no" to behavior that you know in your gut is inappropriate but for which refusal may also carry some real costs. Often, however, what appears to be the easy way out is actually the more costly option.

For example, there was a period in the early days of the Jerusalem fab when we had a pretty serious problem with employee pilferage and theft. "The only way we are going to solve this problem is to install surveillance cameras," my security director told me. I objected to that approach because it felt antithetical to the kind of open organization we were trying to create. Instead of focusing on surveillance, I proposed that we focus on values. We started talking about the theft problem in every employee forum, explaining in detail the costs of pilferage both to our competitiveness and to our values. Within a matter of months, the losses from pilferage declined dramatically.

On another occasion, I received a phone call from an official at Shabak, Israel's internal security service. The agency was setting up a network of people in the business community to supply economic intelligence about companies doing business in Israel, and it wanted Intel to be involved. I unequivocally refused.

It was a risky move. The security establishment in Israel is highly influential, and I'm sure many people would believe that it was our responsibility as loyal Israelis to participate in such a network. But my attitude was, Intel is in the semiconductor business, not the intelligence business. I felt it was inappropriate to be providing such information to the government. What's more, we were an open organization. Anything that smelled of covert activity would be a violation of our values.

When we were negotiating the incentives package for the Qiryat Gat fab with the Israeli government, there was a tough impasse on a couple of the terms. In an effort to improve their leverage, some of the negotiators on the government side leaked details to the Israeli press. The selective leaks put Intel in a bad light and we were pummeled by the press. Things got so bad that I got a message from Intel CEO Craig Barrett saying that he was considering killing the deal.

Some people on my team thought that the solution was to fight fire with fire and start leaking ourselves. But I refused to carry out our negotiations with the government via the press. I simply contacted the leader of the government negotiating team and told him that if the leaks continued, the deal was off. There were no more leaks after that.

Later, after we had built the Qiryat Gat fab, I got a call from the office of Israel's Chief Rabbi. Semiconductor fabs are 24/7 operations. All plants in Intel, no matter where they are located, operate seven days a week. Therefore we needed a permit from the local Rabbinic association to allow the plant to operate on Friday, or *Shabbat*, the Jewish Sabbath. But we were having a hard time getting the permit. Without it, the Ministry of Labor could close us down.

"The Chief Rabbi would like to meet you," the representative from the Chief Rabbi's office told me. "He would like to help you get the permit for Shabbat. He's sure we can work things out." Again, I refused. Either we were going to get the permit or we weren't going to be able to operate legally. But I wasn't going to get involved in any kind of negotiation with the Chief Rabbi, who, as far as I was concerned, had no legitimate role to play in the decisions of a global business organization, and I refused to be dependent on him for any favors. What's more, I calculated that after all the money that the Israeli government had put into the Qiryat Gat fab, the Rabbinate couldn't very well go to the government to close us down. Once they saw that we weren't going to budge, the local Rabbinic association yielded.

In my experience, when you stick to your values, you get rewarded—whatever the risks involved. Indeed, in the spirit of leadership the hard way, often the more difficult or riskier path turns out to be the easiest one in the end. Developing strong values and allowing yourself to be guided by them *simplifies* things. In an uncertain environment, values provide a clear path to follow.

Transparency, Not Purity

In insisting on the importance of staying true to an organization's values, however, I'm not saying that the goal should necessarily be to eliminate any and all value violations. No large complex organization is ever going to be pure as the driven snow. Rather, the goal should be to create a system in which the inevitable value violations that do occur quickly come to people's attention, are identified, and then are corrected. The way to stay true to values is to elevate issues, make people feel comfortable in dealing with them, bring things into the open rather than covering them up. Put another way, the goal isn't purity, it's transparency—and recovery.

This lesson was brought home to me in an experience I had not long after the establishment of the Jerusalem fab. I was traveling to Israel's Ben-Gurion airport to pick up a senior Intel executive who had come from the States to tour the site. Because I was late for his arrival, I left my car parked illegally in the pick-up zone and hurriedly rushed to meet him inside the terminal. Sure enough, when we returned to the car, there was a ticket on the windshield. Later in the day, as we moved from meeting to meeting in the fab,

I quickly stopped by the office of my finance director, explained why I had gotten the ticket, and asked him to take care of it. At the end of the day, he stopped by my office. "Dov, we need to talk," he said. "Your parking ticket is not the company's business. If you violate the parking regulations, then you have to pay for it."

Of course, he was absolutely right. I had been so preoccupied that I hadn't really taken in what I was doing. When he pointed it out to me, I was chagrined that I hadn't lived up to my own values. It is precisely such small, everyday actions—like my assuming that the company would pay my parking ticket—that establishes a general tone. It upset me that, in the rush and pressure of the day, it had been so easy for me to neglect the very values that I talked about all the time.

Yet at the same time I felt enormously gratified that my finance director had felt confident enough to challenge me on it. That was a sign that the Intel Israel culture was working, that we had begun to create an environment where people took the values seriously enough to act on them. Creating such an environment is the biggest achievement you can have. I paid the ticket without argument.

Acknowledging Mistakes

As the parking-ticket example suggests, the importance of values puts a special burden on an organization's leader. On the one hand, you have to try to live up to the values in your own behavior. But even more, you have to be open and honest when you fail—as you inevitably will. The true test of your integrity as a leader is not in the moments when you stay true to the organization's values but, rather, in those when you discover that you have violated them.

It's a key moment of truth. Either you cover up your own inability to live up to the organization's values or you bring it out into the open for people to see. In my experience, covering up only makes things worse, because it's impossible to keep things secret for any length of time. Sooner or later the cover-up fails, things come out, and the result is often increased hypocrisy about values in the organization.

Being open about your own value violations can have many positive effects. For one thing, it tends to humanize you as a leader and strengthen the bond with your people. It shows that you struggle just like they do to live up to the organization's values—and sometimes fall short. It also can lead to a constructive conversation about the inevitable tension of staying true to values in a high-pressure business organization.

Once Intel Israel reached a certain size, we began to have formal orientation and training programs for our new employees. I made sure that one of the orientation sessions was devoted to Intel Israel values. But instead of having the typical lecture or class, I insisted that the session be organized as an informal discussion in which I myself, the organization's leader, would participate. I would come to the meeting, project the organization's values statement onto the screen, and then ask the new employees present (most of whom had already been at the company for six months or so) to identify any values that they believed, based on their experience so far, we were not living up to.

It was never an easy conversation to get started. Often people would hesitate to speak freely. Yet eventually some brave soul would tell a story about something he or she saw, and that would get the ball rolling. Then we would discuss—were these really value violations? If so, how? What were the extenuating circumstances? How did we think various participants saw the situation from their perspective? What should you do about it if you confront a similar situation?

Once I arrived at one of these orientation sessions at the Qiryat Gat fab about half an hour late. As I was entering the site, I found myself thinking about an old Israeli saying, "*Menahel lo marcher hu rak mit'akev*" (A manager is never late, only delayed). How convenient, how self-protective for the manager, I thought. So when I walked into the room, the first thing I said was, "This is a session on Intel Israel values. And by arriving late, I have violated at least three of the values we espouse. I haven't shown respect for people. I didn't display a results orientation. And I definitely wasn't committed to quality."

Acknowledging my own failure to live up to the organization's values made the conversation very real. We talked about how difficult it can be to stay true to our values given the daily demands and pressures of the business, yet how important it was to the long-term success and survival of Intel Israel. In my opinion, it was one of the best sessions on values that we had ever had.

Maintaining the Tension Between Values and Behavior

The battle to establish high ethical standards in an organization never ends. Again, the goal should not be some impossible purity but rather a willingness to embrace the necessary tension that making values real entails. People don't like it when there is a gap between their behavior and the values they espouse. On the one hand, they are right: the ultimate goal is to align behavior with values. But sometimes, in an effort to eliminate that gap, people rush too quickly to close it. Put simply, they change the values, not the behavior.

Let me conclude with an example of what I mean. Not long before I retired, I found myself in a meeting with my senior staff to revisit the language of the organization's values statement, something that we did routinely every few years. One of the values on our list was "integrity without compromises." A number of people at the meeting thought that definitely needed editing. Put simply, they wanted to remove the phrase "without compromises."

They worried that this strong language promised more than the organization could deliver. The fact was, we were continuously finding ourselves in somewhat compromising situations, dealing with boundary issues for which the imperatives of integrity seemed to conflict with good business practice. One manager gave the example of how we handled overtime pay. There was some language in Israeli labor law, albeit somewhat vague, mandating employers to pay extra for overtime. But at Intel Israel, we followed the U.S. practice of distinguishing between exempt (that is, supervisory) and non-exempt (that is, hourly) employees. For the non-exempt hourly employees, we of course did pay overtime. But for the exempt group, who were on salary, we didn't even keep track of the hours they worked. Their responsibility was to get the job done, and from the perspective of the company, it didn't matter if they worked more than eight hours a day—or less.

It wasn't at all clear that our policies violated the law. Certainly no one, neither employees nor government officials, had ever complained. But the critics argued that it was a bit of a gray area. Weren't we perhaps compromising our integrity? Better to avoid the issue by simply eliminating the "without compromises" language. "Isn't 'integrity' good enough?" they asked.

I had a different perspective. The fact that we constantly faced situations that might compromise our integrity wasn't a reason to eliminate the "without compromises" language. Quite the contrary: it was a reason to keep it. If we eliminated those two words, we ran the risk of becoming complacent. We would start taking such situations for granted instead of continuously questioning them and asking whether we were in fact doing the right thing. Emphasizing the ideal of "integrity without compromises" created a tension. It forced us to think about things and to address them pragmatically. Who knows? Maybe we should reconsider our policy. Or perhaps we should be working to get the government to revise the law.

I refused to make the change. The values statement remained as written. I suspect it probably made some of my people nervous. Could we really live up to the value as written? I wasn't so worried, because that was exactly the question that I wanted them to keep asking.

7

BOOTSTRAPPING LEADERSHIP

At the beginning of this book I argued that the essentials of leadership are more akin to wisdom than they are to knowledge. Because leadership is not really a skill, it cannot really be taught. Rather than hoping to learn in the classroom or from some training program how to lead, aspiring leaders need to take on the hard work of bootstrapping leadership—that is, learning how to lead by *doing* it. In the body of the book, I have tried to show how this process played itself out in my own career as I pursued my life project of creating a new high-tech business in Israel and taking it from the periphery to the very center of a major global corporation.

It's all well and good to say "learn by doing." But how does a potential leader learn *from* doing? In this concluding chapter, I want to describe four resources that an aspiring leader can use to learn how to lead. Reading these pages won't necessarily turn you into a leader any more than any other book on the subject will. But they just might give you some ideas for where to start your own bootstrapping once you finish this book.

Staying True to Your Passion

No leader can be effective who does not identify 100 percent with the organization's mission. A leader doesn't have the luxury to be equivocal. You have to make sure that your personal mission and the organizational mission are perfectly aligned. After the First Gulf War, for example, someone at Intel Israel said to me, "You were behaving as if your *own* personal survival was at stake, not just the survival of Intel Israel." It's true, because by that time I had completely identified with Intel Israel and its future.

Because this identification between leader and organization is so important, it's critical for you as an aspiring leader to identify your passion—what really drives you—and to stay true to that passion through the course of your career. If you do, you will find that this passion is a powerful resource for guiding you through the challenges of leadership the hard way.

There are many sources for identifying your passion. One is your early life experiences. Your fundamental approach to leadership is set long before you ever reach a position of authority. In my own case, the experiences of my World War II childhood, of being an observer of and participant in the Berkeley counterculture of the 1960s, and of developing a breakthrough innovation in the computer industry with my invention of the EPROM all profoundly shaped the kind of leader I wanted—and was able—to become. Fortunately, these experiences nurtured an approach to leadership that turned out to be highly effective in the fast-moving and highly turbulent economy in which I found myself. Aspiring leaders need to understand the origins of their individual leadership styles and how those origins map to the specific challenges of business competition today.

Another key part of staying true to your passion is to define, as early as possible, a vision or mission to which you want to dedicate yourself. It doesn't matter how unrealistic or even crazy that vision might appear at the time. Even the vaguest plan—like my early desire to "bring something back" to Israel—has the value of being a reference point that orients would-be leaders and helps guide their choices, actions, and decisions.

Over time, as you gain experience, the vision will become more concrete. At that point, one of the most important ways to stay true to your passion will be knowing when to say no. Once you gain some success, it is extremely easy to get swamped by opportunities that may seem attractive at the moment but don't really take you where you want to go. To avoid getting knocked off track, it's important to always be asking, will this opportunity take me closer to my goal?

For example, at the time of my conversation with Andy Grove about Engineer A and Engineer B, I dimly realized that my passion wasn't really to become an American-style manager at Intel, that I wanted to do something else: to create something in Israel. Saying no to the role that Andy was holding out for me was a way of saying yes to my core passion, even though I didn't quite know then how I would realize it.

Finally, as a leader you must learn how to renew your passion over time. In the course of an entire career there are bound to be times when your passion will flag. You will lose touch with the mission that energized you before. Or you may feel that you have already accomplished what you set out to do. That is the time to reflect on the original passion that had brought you to this point and, if possible, to reframe your mission so that it puts you back in touch with that passion.

I'll give you an example from my own experience. By the time I approached retirement, I felt like my dream—to bring something back from the United States and build a new field of industry and technology in Israel—was largely fulfilled. Intel Israel was well established and thriving. And a dynamic high-tech industry had grown up around it, making Israel a genuine global center for high tech.

Yet now I realize that my mission wasn't really over. More recently I have found myself engaged with the critical question of what it will take for Israel's high-tech sector to survive and thrive into the future. And that concern has led to an unanticipated encounter with Israeli politics and the conflicts of the Middle East.

At the time of the Oslo Accords (1993), there was a lot of hope that high tech could be a powerful focus for future collaboration between Israelis and Palestinians and a driver of economic development in the entire region. But as of this writing, with the prospect of peace growing increasingly dim, I worry that the worsening political instability in the region is a serious strategic threat to high tech's future. The current status quo in Israel, which combines extraordinary economic dynamism with extreme political stasis, is neither acceptable nor sustainable. Unless Israel can find its way to a definitive settlement with the Palestinians and the broader Arab world, Israel's high-tech industry won't be fully secure. Trying to address that challenge is turning out to be a new phase of my mission and a new focus of my lifelong passion.

The Invisible Mentor

In ancient times those in search of wisdom sought out a guru. Today we talk about *mentors*. Mentorship has become a big theme in the management literature in recent years, and many organizations have established formal mentorship programs. Having read this far, you won't be surprised to learn that I'm skeptical of their value. A lot of these mentorship programs, much like formal leadership programs, are pretty formulaic. Sure, they can be useful in helping new executives enter smoothly into the organizational culture and develop networks with colleagues and superiors. But they don't really turn people into leaders.

Other experts emphasize close personal relationships with senior leaders that last over many years. For example, in his recent book *True North*, former Medtronic CEO Bill George argues that what many aspiring leaders fail to recognize is "the importance of the two-way relationship with their mentors. *Lasting relationships must flow both ways.* The best mentoring interactions spark mutual learning, exploration of similar values, and shared enjoyment."[1] Such two-way relationships are great—if you can find them. But not every aspiring leader is so fortunate as to forge such a close personal relationship with a senior leader.

I want to suggest a different approach; call it *invisible mentorship*. As an aspiring leader, you shouldn't wait to be assigned a mentor or simply hope for someone in a senior leadership position to tap you on the shoulder and take you under his or her wing. Be more active: choose your own invisible mentor, someone whose behavior you study from afar. It doesn't really matter whether that individual knows you are doing this or not.

In my career, the most valuable mentors were individuals who weren't playing the formal role and didn't know I was using them in that way. I was extremely fortunate, of course, to work at a company that had some of the best business leaders of the late twentieth century. Long before anyone was talking about human capital, Intel founder Robert Noyce understood the centrality of people to an innovation-based business. And I will always be grateful to Gordon Moore for his extraordinary technical vision and for his willingness to take risks and place big bets—whether on the EPROM as a revolutionary new product or on Israel as a place where Intel could successfully do business. But the individual who, more than any other, shaped me as a leader was, as you've probably gathered by now, Andy Grove. For many years, Andy functioned as my invisible mentor, even though neither he nor I was really aware of it at the time.

I first met Andy in 1965, when I was a graduate student at Berkeley and he interviewed me for a job in his lab at Fairchild Semiconductor. In some respects our relationship got off to a rocky start. Although Andy offered me a job, I chose to work in another Fairchild lab, not his. And when Andy taught a course for new employees on solid-state physics at what was to me the ungodly hour of 7:00 AM, I was the one who complained about his giving us quizzes before we were even awake (I once overhead him complaining to a colleague about this kid who had barely arrived and was already giving him trouble). Later, of course, after I had joined Intel, invented the EPROM, and then decided to give it all up to travel in Africa, it was Andy who made it clear that he thought the proper thing for me to do was to stay on and see the prototype through to a finished product.

Andy and I had an odd relationship. We knew each other, of course, but our relationship was always somewhat distant. In all my years at Intel, I never reported directly to him. I was always one or two levels down in the hierarchy and, once I moved to Israel, thousands of miles away. Despite the widespread belief inside Intel that we were in constant communication, I would see him, at most, maybe three or four times a year. In the roughly thirty-five years that we worked together, we never had a single in-depth personal conversation. For example, we never discussed our Jewish roots or our parallel experiences as Jewish children in Nazi-occupied Europe during World War II.[2]

On the other hand, over the years Andy and I developed a highly productive working relationship. My impression always was that whenever I asked for a meeting to discuss some new project or initiative for Intel Israel, Andy already half-knew where I was going and what I was up to. And although we didn't always agree, I always found him remarkably open and extremely supportive of what I was trying to do.

This openness, which was even a kind of generosity, was captured for me by an incident that happened after I left Africa to spend six months at Intel in Silicon Valley before finally returning to Israel. Just before I left Santa Clara for Israel, where I would teach at Hebrew University, Andy threw a farewell party for me at his house. At one point I found myself sitting in an extremely comfortable rocking chair on his front porch. "What a great chair," I told him.

"Do you want it?" he asked immediately. My wife was pregnant at the time, and I answered, "My wife would love it."

"Take it," he said. That chair was one of the few artifacts that I brought back with me from Silicon Valley to Israel.

Andy's support gave me enormous leverage inside Intel, and I was happy to exploit it. He was the Intel senior executive responsible for operations, so he was always the key decision maker for many of the initiatives that I wanted to undertake. Whenever I got involved in a confrontation with colleagues, they would have to be careful because they thought that if push came to shove, I might get Andy involved. I tried not to abuse our relationship, but on a few critical occasions—the conflicts over Intel Israel's no-transfer rule, for example, or the bake-off that led to the decision to build the Jerusalem fab—I didn't hesitate to use it.

My relationship with Andy bothered some people at Intel. They thought I was short-circuiting established lines of authority.

"The problem with you, Dov," Andy once told me, relatively late in my career at Intel, "is that nobody knows whom you report to." He was right. Of course, I did have a formal reporting relationship. But I never let it stop me or constrain my own sense of my power or room for maneuver. I treated the Intel hierarchy like a "fuzzy network" in which I had many, many points of interaction. Some were based on formal reporting relationships, but others were based on a shared history, personal relationships, and practical alliances that I had built up over the years.

To be sure, I had the distinct advantage of being a country manager in an operation that was far away, physically, from corporate headquarters. Yet a lot of country managers I knew at Intel seemed to define their role as dependent on corporate. Early on, I made a conscious decision to take the opposite tack—that is, to assume that I had the freedom to act, and then to let the chips fall where they may.

Something about the very distance in my relationship with Andy seemed to invest small things with large significance. For example, when I was a young manager at Intel Israel, I sent Andy a five-page proposal for shifting the Jerusalem fab production line from memories to microprocessors. He returned it, unread, with a stamp reading "Please respect my time." His message: the proposal was way too long. He wanted one page, not five. Grove's request— "Please respect my time"—had an enormous impact on me. Indeed, it sparked a lifelong reflection on how leaders use—and abuse— their time that eventually led to my focus on freeing up time, which I described in Chapter Five.

I learned a lot of things from Andy over the years: the importance of integrity and modesty, of finding and following your own passion, of paying attention to detail (not my strongest suit, I admit), of not taking no for an answer but instead always asking "Why not?" Indeed, I would say that to the degree I had a model for leadership the hard way, Andy was it. But again, his example worked on me only from afar. In all the years we worked together, we never discussed it.

Recently, I was surprised to learn that Andy had had an invisible mentor of his own. In his recent biography of Grove, Harvard Business School professor Richard Tedlow describes how Charlie Sporck, the legendary semiconductor manufacturing manager and founder of National Semiconductor, was a key role model for Grove in his transition from scientist to operations manager. Sporck, Grove told Tedlow, seemed to epitomize "the operations guy that I aspired to become. Without my knowing him particularly well at the time, he became my role model. He cast a big shadow over my life without ever knowing that he did so."[3] Although the situations are obviously different, I could say pretty much the same thing about Andy: he cast a big shadow over my life as a leader without ever really knowing that he did so.

My point: no aspiring leader has to wait to be assigned a mentor or has to depend on developing a close personal relationship with one. Look around you. Choose someone whose leadership style you relate to and admire. Study that person closely. It will help you bootstrap your own leadership capacity.

Becoming a "Reflective Practitioner"

A would-be pilot always has the option of using a flight simulator. But there is no effective way to simulate leading an organization. Instead, aspiring leaders face the difficult challenge of learning from their own experience at the very moment that they are experiencing it.

This is different from what usually passes for learning from experience in the business world. Most management education is built around the ideas of the success story (think of the typical case studies produced at places like the Harvard Business School). More recently, some management thinkers have begun to focus on the idea of learning from failures as well.[4] But both success stories and failure stories suffer from two critical limitations. First, they are ex post facto—that is, they tell the moral of the story after you already know how the story ends. And second, they are inevitably one step removed from the would-be leader's own experience. The kind of learning that is really of value is the learning that happens in the moment. It's the kind of systematic reflection on one's own experience that organizational theorist Donald Schön captured in his term "the reflective practitioner."[5]

In my experience, there are a variety of ways to develop this capacity to reflect systematically on one's own experience in the moment. One is to realize that although leadership is a public act, to be effective a leader also has to have an active inner life. In Chapter Five, I described some of the ways of stimulating habits of reflection that worked for me: freeing up time, daydreaming, intuitive decision making, and the like.

But another key aspect is to build systematic reflection into your everyday activity. I think the organizations that do this best are found in the military: the "after action review" has become a routine activity after every military engagement. Once, rather late in my tenure at Intel Israel, I hosted a group of officers from an Israeli air force base in the Negev at our fab in Qiryat Gat. They were interested in the practices that we had put in place to ensure quality and continuous improvement in our manufacturing process. But for me the most interesting moment in the meeting came when the officers described a practice of their own. It was a system for analyzing what they called "near accidents"—that is, any close calls between maneuvering planes that could easily have led to disaster but, in the end, did not. Later, I visited the base and observed the intensive video analysis that pilots did of their near accidents.

I am intrigued by this concept of the near accident as a potentially useful analogy for leaders-to-be to encourage learning from experience. Anything a leader does consists of multiple near accidents in which success or failure hangs in the balance. Take for example my invention of the EPROM. In retrospect it was definitely a success story. But any number of things could have gone wrong—and nearly did—along the way. For example, it was a real challenge getting my colleagues to see the potential value of my new approach to designing a semiconductor memory. It was like nothing they had seen before, and they had a hard time getting their minds around it. What's more, when I first came up with the concept, I had yet to demonstrate it definitively, so it was easy to dismiss as a crazy idea. What I learned from that experience was the absolute importance of persistence, of insisting on the impossible, even in the face of disagreement and resistance. And doing so gave me the confidence to follow my dream no matter how "unrealistic" it might appear and no matter where it might lead.

I learned all this haphazardly, in retrospect, almost by chance. I think that with a little effort aspiring leaders could engage in such learning *systematically*—by regularly exposing their experiences to some version of an after action review.

Learning from Your People

A prominent theme in this book has been the imperative of leaders to forge close bonds with their people. That close bond is essential for getting an organization to meet the demands of leadership the hard way. But it also has another advantage: a close relationship with your people can give you a tremendous resource for bootstrapping your leadership capabilities.

There are a variety of ways that an aspiring leader can develop that close bond. In previous chapters, for example, I've discussed the importance of the leader being present to the organization—in the way I tried to be present during the First Gulf War or when we instituted the 10 percent pay cut. It is precisely at difficult moments, when unpalatable decisions have to be made, that you need to expose yourself to your people's reactions and input. The less you insulate yourself from these reactions, the more you learn, and the better a leader you become.

Another way, frankly, is through self-criticism—not being afraid to expose one's own mistakes to the organization, as I did when I discussed the ways that I was violating our values by coming late to the values training session. A would-be leader needs to get comfortable with the idea that his own actions will be exposed to the organization. Don't be afraid to reveal yourself, to talk about your failures and your mistakes. It will humanize you in the eyes of your people and build a stronger bond. What's more, it will encourage honest feedback and openness throughout the organization—organizational characteristics that are essential for leadership the hard way to work effectively.

A third way—again, much discussed in previous chapters—is by welcoming dissent. It can be difficult, sometimes, to navigate all the various points of view and to distinguish genuine dissent from simple excuses. But the more you create an atmosphere in which all points of view are welcome, the more you will be empowering your people to contribute to your own capacity to lead.

Finally, leaders form close bonds with their people by using their own behavior strategically. Aspiring leaders should get in the habit of thinking of their actions as a form of communication. Remember, the organization is always watching you. What are the lessons you want to impart through your behavior?

When you do all these things, you will find that not only does your own influence grow, but you will also have created a two-way communication with your people that will help you grow and develop as a leader.

To become a truly effective leader, of course, it isn't enough just to bootstrap your own leadership capacity. You also have to bootstrap the next generation of leaders. A lot of companies these days are setting up formal succession-planning programs. But what I am talking about is so much more than succession planning. In effect, leaders are planning for succession every day—in the way they function as role models, in the way they communicate their decisions, in the mistakes they make and how they react to them. It is through everyday behavior that aspiring leaders institutionalize their leadership approach in the organization.

At Intel Israel, many of the decisions I made regarding people—the no-transfer rule, recruiting a more diverse workforce, lateral transfers among managers—all had to do with expanding the pool of potential next-generation leaders and providing them with the experiences they needed to develop their own leadership capacities. How they responded to the challenges I set for them taught me who had the capacity to develop into a genuine leader and who did not. Over time I was able develop a cadre of leaders that were empowered to make important decisions without my direct involvement. Once I had achieved this, succession planning more or less took care of itself.

In the process, one of the things I learned is that leaders are found in the strangest places. Often the best candidates turn out to be people from outside the mainstream—the misfits, the critics, sometimes even the naysayers—who at first glance one would never expect would have leadership potential. So be prepared to look for new leaders in unexpected places and to give them the opportunity they need to bootstrap their own learning. You'll become a better leader as a result.

Passion, mentors, in-the-moment reflection, people—these are some of the key resources that an aspiring leader can use to bootstrap leadership. What you will learn from using them is not so much the skills of leadership but the wisdom of leadership: that ineffable but essential dimension of leadership that cannot really be taught.

But in the end you will have to find your own way, and, no doubt, it will be different from my own. You will have to take the principles outlined in this book and make them come alive in a way that makes sense for you, given your own history, personality, and organizational context. When you do, you will have embarked on the lifelong journey of becoming a self-taught leader—just as I did more than thirty years ago.

Epilogue:
Knowing When to Let Go

The ultimate act of leadership is knowing when to let go. In my experience, many leaders, even quite successful ones, stay on far too long in positions of authority. They don't step down until they realize that they have begun to fail. But the damage to the organization is already done, because by the time a leader recognizes that he or she is failing, chances are it has already been the case for many years. Better to leave at a point of time that may seem to be too early. No individual is indispensable. Sometimes, leaving is the most effective act of leadership there is.

In 2001, I retired from Intel and let go of the reins of leadership at Intel Israel. I left because I had begun to feel like I was repeating myself. Often, in meetings with my staff and subordinates, I found myself thinking "I've heard all these questions before." And I distrusted my sense that I also knew all the answers. When you get to the point that you are flying on autopilot most of the time, it is high time to land.

People were surprised at my decision. I was leaving at the height of our achievement, much as I did when I first left Intel after inventing the EPROM to go teach in Africa. Many people thought it was "too soon." Some even wondered whether Intel Israel could continue to succeed without me running interference for the organization with Intel corporate.

I wasn't worried. I felt it was time for the organization to have new leaders who would bring fresh perspectives on Intel Israel's challenges and opportunities. I saw my retirement as yet another way to break through the complacency that can develop in any successful organization, to force the organization to stay on its toes and to step up and take responsibility for Intel Israel's future survival.

My attitude was, I had created the Intel Israel culture and institutionalized a distinctive style of leadership; now it was time for me to get out of the way. If I stayed to the very last minute, tried to maintain my control, the new generation of leaders wouldn't be able to express themselves, to take on more responsibility, and to become leaders in their own right. And I was confident that they were ready to lead.

Subsequent events proved me right. Intel Israel's actions during the 2006 summer war between Israel and Hezbollah (which, for the Haifa design center, was far more dangerous than anything we faced in the First Gulf War) demonstrated that the organization is still insisting on survival. The development of the innovative Core 2 Duo family of low-power microprocessors, introduced in 2006, showed that Intel Israel continues to lead against the current. And the 2005 announcement that Intel would invest $3.5 billion to build a new state-of-the-art semiconductor fab in Qiryat Gat (the biggest construction project in the history of the state of Israel, the new fab is taking shape, as I write, next door to the existing plant) illustrated that Intel Israel is still leveraging random opportunities to win the global competition for investment.

I made a clean break when I left Intel Israel. Indeed, the first time I returned to an Intel Israel site was some six years later, when I was in the midst of writing this book. For years, people would ask me, "When are you coming back?" They still do. But it was clear to me that there was no need. They are doing far better than I could have done if I were still around.

Another question I often hear from former colleagues is "So, what are you doing these days?" Usually I respond, "Trying to figure out what I am going to do when I grow up!" The real answer is, spending time at my vacation home in the Dolomite Mountains of northeastern Italy, a country and culture that I love for its delightful randomness and flair for improvisation that is very much in the spirit of leadership the hard way; writing this book to capture and share my thinking about the lessons of my life and my career; and looking for new creative ways to push my ideas beyond the realm of business and to address the crisis of leadership in our world.

Back in the 1990s, when we were looking for a site for what would become the first Qiryat Gat fab, I developed a passion for Israel's south—a passion that continues to this day. Israel's first prime minister, David Ben-Gurion, was convinced that the future of the country would be found there—so much so that when he retired from politics he went to live at Kibbutz Sde Boker, near Wadi Hawarim, deep in the Negev Desert. One of my retirement projects is to create what I call a "center for alternative thinking" on a high plateau above Sde Boker. The purpose of the center is to expose the next generation of Israelis to unconventional ways of seeing the world and to promote innovation and creativity. It will be a place where people from all walks of life can come together to explore fresh solutions to some of the most intractable problems facing our society. What will it take to finally realize Ben-Gurion's vision for the development of the south of Israel? How can we meet the challenges of Israel's failing educational system? And, perhaps most important, what are the alternatives to the by now thoroughly exhausted paradigms of "security" and "terrorism" in our relations with the Palestinians?

Some people think the idea is crazy. Why would anyone want to come to the middle of nowhere just to discuss tough, and maybe even impossible, problems? But I'm used to such skepticism. Thirty-five years ago, who would have imagined that the world's most advanced microprocessors would be designed and built in the Middle East?

As I've said many times, leadership the hard way means not taking no for an answer.

If you can't go through the door, go through the window.

Sometimes the best way to survive a thunderstorm is to fly right through it.

Notes

Introduction

1. See *360°: The Merrill Lynch Leadership Magazine*, inaugural issue published Sept. 2006 at http://mag1.olivesoftware .com/am/welcome/360TheMerrillLynchLeadershipMagazine/ Dec2006/
2. See, for example, the description of Gonzaga University's Ph.D. in Leadership Studies at http://www.gonzaga.edu/ Academics/Colleges+and+Schools/School+of+Professional +Studies/Ph.D.+-+Leadership+Studies/default.asp
3. Wolfgang Langewiesche, *Stick and Rudder: An Explanation of the Art of Flying* (McGraw-Hill, Inc., 1972), p. 3.
4. Andrew S. Grove, *Only the Paranoid Survive* (Doubleday Currency, 1996), p. 5.
5. See Clayton M. Christensen, *The Innovator's Dilemma: How New Technologies Cause Great Firms to Fail* (Harvard Business School Press, 1997).
6. Langewiesche, *Stick and Rudder*, p. 5.
7. See AnnaLee Saxenian, *The New Argonauts: Regional Advantage in a Global Economy* (Harvard University Press, 2006).
8. As quoted in *A Revolution in Progress: A History of Intel to Date* (Intel Corporation, 1984), p. 22.
9. See Warren Bennis and Robert Thomas, *Geeks and Geezers: How Eras, Values, and Defining Moments Shape Leaders* (Harvard Business School Press, 2002).

Chapter One

1. Grove, *Only the Paranoid Survive*, p. 3.
2. These figures come from Bob Moore, *Victims and Survivors: The Nazi Persecution of the Jews in the Netherlands, 1940–1945* (Arnold, 1997), pp. 146, 164–165.

Chapter Two

1. See Ed Michaels, Helen Handfield-Jones, and Beth Axelrod, *The War for Talent* (Harvard Business School Press, 2001).
2. See Ian King, "Intel's Israelis Make Chip to Rescue Company From Profit Plunge," *Bloomberg News*, Mar. 27, 2007.

Chapter Three

1. Robert A. Burgelman, *Strategy Is Destiny: How Strategy-Making Shapes a Company's Future* (Free Press, 2002), p. 90.
2. Tim Jackson, *Inside Intel: Andy Grove and the Rise of the World's Most Powerful Chip Company* (Dutton, 1997), p. 106.

Chapter Four

1. The statistics in this section are from "The Gulf Crisis in Israel: A War for the Age of Uncertainty," *Israel Yearbook* and *Almanac 1991/92* (IBR Translations/Documentation Limited, 1992).
2. See Dov Frohman, "Leadership Under Fire," *Harvard Business Review*, Dec. 2006, pp. 124–131.

Chapter Five

1. Marcus Aurelius, *Meditations*, Book IV (Dover Publications, 1997), p. 23.
2. For recent reviews of this research, see Robin M. Hogarth, *Educating Intuition* (University of Chicago Press, 2001); David

G. Myers, *Intuition: Its Powers and Perils* (Yale University Press, 2002); and Malcolm Gladwell, *Blink: The Power of Thinking Without Thinking* (Little, Brown and Co., 2005).

3. For the classic description of the role of tacit knowledge in innovation, see Ikujiro Nonaka and Hirotaka Takeuchi, *The Knowledge-Creating Company: How Japanese Companies Create the Dynamics of Innovation* (Oxford University Press, 1995).

4. As quoted in Myers, *Intuition*, p. 1.

5. For a comprehensive set of guidelines for educating intuition, see Hogarth, *Educating Intuition*, pp. 207–212.

Chapter Six

1. For a by now classic statement on this issue, see Robert Howard, "Values Make the Company: An Interview with Robert Haas," *Harvard Business Review*, Sept.–Oct. 1990, p. 134.

Chapter Seven

1. Bill George, with Peter Sims, *True North: Discover Your Authentic Leadership* (Jossey-Bass, A Warren Bennis Book, 2007), pp. 120–121.

2. For Grove's experiences during the war, see Andrew S. Grove, *Swimming Across: A Memoir* (Warner, 2001); and Richard S. Tedlow, *Andy Grove: The Life and Times of an American* (Portfolio Penguin, 2006).

3. Tedlow, *Andy Grove*, p. 151.

4. See, for example, Sydney Finkelstein, *Why Smart Executives Fail* (Penguin Putnam, 2003); and Jeffrey A. Sonnenfeld and Andrew J. Ward, *Firing Back: How Great Leaders Rebound After Career Disasters* (Harvard Business School Press, 2007).

5. See Donald Schön, *The Reflective Practitioner: How Professionals Think in Action* (Basic Books, 1983).

Acknowledgments

This book is the product of a lifetime's work and learning, and many people have contributed to my perspective on leadership along the way. I would like to thank, first, all my colleagues at Fairchild Semiconductor and at Intel Corporation with whom I shared the challenges of leadership over more than three decades; in particular, the late Bob Seeds, my first boss in the Digital Electronics department at Fairchild's R&D laboratories; Les Vadasz, my first boss at Intel; and Intel's former CEO and current chairman, Craig Barrett.

I also want to acknowledge the extraordinary contribution and achievement of Intel's founders, Gordon Moore and the late Robert Noyce. Not only did they support me in my endeavors from the early days of the development of the EPROM, but they also created an organization and a culture in which I was continually encouraged to take risks, pursue my dreams, and bring them to fruition. They were truly inspiring leaders.

As the preceding pages make clear, I owe a special debt of gratitude to Andy Grove. From that first moment when I turned down Andy's offer to work in his lab at Fairchild, Andy has been an important figure in my life. It was Andy, more than any other single individual, who made possible the creation of Intel Israel. I could not have achieved what I did without his support, advice, and, sometimes, criticism. He is my model for leadership the hard way.

I would also like to thank all my former colleagues at Intel Israel and, in particular, the first generation of leaders who helped build the organization: the late Moshe Balog, Marek Sternheim, Eli Porat, Rafi Nave, Alex Kornhauser, and Dadi Perlmutter.

When I first began to think about writing this book, I approached the well-known Israeli writer and *Yedioth Ahronoth* columnist Meir Shalev. I would like to thank Meir not only for encouraging me to pursue my project but also for having the good sense not to tell me just how difficult writing a book would be.

My Jerusalem friend Bernard Avishai, author of *The Tragedy of Zionism* and contributing editor at the *Harvard Business Review*, read an unwieldy early version of my manuscript and helped me figure out what to do with it. I want to thank Bernie especially for the delicacy and finesse with which he persuaded me that I needed a writing partner and for putting me in touch with one.

This book would not have been possible without the engagement, skills, and experienced counsel of that writer, Robert Howard. I was always amazed by the way that Bob would completely change what I had originally written and yet in the process succeed in capturing exactly what I wanted to say. I want to thank him for what has been an efficient—and extremely enjoyable—collaboration. I will remember fondly our working sessions in the Dolomites, Boston, and Jerusalem. (A special thanks to Bob and his wife Leslie Schneider for their hospitality during my visit to Boston in the summer of 2006.)

I also want to thank the various editors who have helped shepherd the book into publication. Diane Coutu, senior editor at the *Harvard Business Review*, championed an early version of Chapter Four and expertly guided it into the pages of that important resource for managers and leaders. Susan Williams saw the potential of this project and has made a wonderful home for it at Jossey-Bass. And Rob Brandt has ably managed the editorial process. I am especially grateful to Warren Bennis, distinguished professor of business administration and founding chairman of the Leadership Institute at the University of Southern California's Marshall School of Business, for choosing this book as a title in the Warren Bennis Signature series at Jossey-Bass. My thanks to Warren for this singular honor.

My heartfelt gratitude and appreciation also go out to my family—my wife, Eilat, my son, Eran, and my daughter, Lora. For many years, their sacrifices allowed me to pursue with unstinting focus and engagement my passion to create Intel Israel. They have graciously put up with my daydreaming and my risk taking (including in that thunderstorm over the Peloponnese!). And they have read and commented on early versions of my manuscript. They have been partners throughout this venture.

Finally, I have chosen to dedicate this book to the memory of my three sets of parents who, at great sacrifice in a dark and dangerous time, helped launch me on my life's path: my birth parents, Abraham and Feijga Frohman; my temporary wartime parents, Antonie and Jenneke Van Tilborgh; and my adoptive parents in Israel, Lea and Moshe Bentchkowsky.

The Authors

Dov Frohman

Dov Frohman is a pioneer of the global corporation. A former executive at Intel Corporation, he was the founder and general manager of Intel Israel, the company's operations in Israel. For nearly thirty years, he created and led a highly successful organization in one of the most demanding and competitive industries and in one of the most dangerous regions of the world.

During his time at Intel, Mr. Frohman was a leading innovator in the semiconductor industry. An Israeli citizen, he was trained in electrical engineering at the Israel Institute of Technology (Technion) in Haifa, Israel, and received his Ph.D. in electrical engineering and computer science from the University of California at Berkeley. As a new employee at Intel, he invented the EPROM—the first reprogrammable read-only semiconductor memory—an innovation that Intel founder Gordon Moore has termed "as important in the development of the microcomputer industry as the microprocessor itself." For this singular achievement, Mr. Frohman received the IEEE Jack Morton Award in 1982 and the prestigious IEEE Edison Medal in 2008.

Mr. Frohman spent most of his career building Intel Israel into a flagship of the Intel Corporation and a cornerstone of the Israeli high-tech economy. He helped found Intel Israel in 1974, became its general manager in 1981, and ran the organization until his retirement in 2001. In recognition of his scientific and technical achievements and of his contributions to the development of Israel's high-technology sector, Mr. Frohman was awarded the Israel Prize for Engineering and Technology in 1991.

During his long and illustrious career, Mr. Frohman also served as visiting professor at the University of Science and Technology in Kumasi, Ghana, and as professor of applied physics at the Hebrew University in Jerusalem, Israel, where he directed the School of Applied Science and Technology.

Today, Mr. Frohman divides his time between his two homes, one in Jerusalem and one in Selva di Cadore in the Dolomite region of Italy.

Robert Howard

Robert Howard is a veteran writer on work, technology, and management. He is the author of *Brave New Workplace* (The Viking Press, Elisabeth Sifton Books, 1985) and the editor of *The Learning Imperative: Managing People for Continuous Innovation* (Harvard Business School Press, 1993).

Mr. Howard's writing has appeared in a number of national publications including the *Harvard Business Review*, MIT's *Technology Review*, the *New York Times Book Review*, and *The New Republic*. He has been the recipient of an Award for Distinguished Investigative Reporting from Investigative Reporters and Editors (IRE) and the Jack London Award from the United Steelworkers Press Association.

Mr. Howard has been a senior editor at *Technology Review* and at the *Harvard Business Review*. He also worked for ten years as director of idea development at The Boston Consulting Group, a major international management consulting firm.

Mr. Howard is a summa cum laude graduate of Amherst College and has done graduate work in sociology and history at the University of Cambridge in England and the Ecole Normale Supérieure in Paris, France. He has been a visiting scholar in the Program on Science, Technology, and Society at the Massachusetts Institute of Technology and an affiliate scholar at the Boston Psychoanalytic Institute.

Mr. Howard lives in Newton, Massachusetts.

Index